Choosing Partnership,
❦ Sharing Ministry

Choosing Partnership, ∞ Sharing Ministry

A Vision for New Spiritual Community

Marcia Barnes Bailey

THE ALBAN INSTITUTE

Herndon, Virginia
www.alban.org

The Alban Institute
2121 Cooperative Way, Suite 100
Herndon, VA 20171

Scripture quotations, unless otherwise noted, are reprinted with permission from the Inclusive New Testament, copyright © 1996, by Priests for Equality/Quixote Center, Inc.

Scripture quotations noted as NRSV are from the New Revised Standard Version of the Bible, © 1989, Division of Christian Education of the National Council of Churches of Christ in the United States of America, and are used by permission.

Cover design by Spark Design, LLC.

Cover photo by Phil Hulme.

Library of Congress Cataloging-in-Publication Data

Bailey, Marcia.
  Choosing partnership, sharing ministry : a vision for new spiritual community / Marcia Bailey.
    p. cm.
  Includes bibliographical references.
  ISBN 978-1-56699-343-2
  1. Communities—Religious aspects—Christianity. 2. Church work.
3. Fellowship—Religious aspects—Christianity. I. Title.

  BV625.B35 2007
  253--dc22

                                    2007008445

    11   10   09   08   07   UG   1   2   3   4   5

To Marcus, a true partner in the vision,
and to all who dare to live the reign of God.

Contents

Foreword, *Marcus C. Pomeroy*   ix

Preface   xiii

Acknowledgements   xvii

1   Imagining Alternatives   1

2   The Gift of Interdependence   17

3   Power in Partnership   33
    Redefining Relationships

4   New Spiritual Community   49

5   Living into the Vision   67

Appendix A   Partnership   91
              Vocabulary and Vision for Congregational Life
              An Adult Learning Curriculum

Appendix B   Web Visions   113
              Leadership as Community
              A Sermon Series

Notes   149

Annotated Bibliography   151

Foreword

⌘P artnership, collaborative ministry, and nonhierarchical pastoral leadership are all descriptions of what Marcia Bailey
and I created during the eleven years we served together as the
pastoral team at Central Baptist Church (CBC) of Wayne,
Pennsylvania.

As Marcia makes clear, both of us came to partnership from
our own experience of struggle and transformation. I was invited
to the hope of an organic, non hierarchical partnership through
the path of contemplative spirituality. In my previous 28 years
of ministry I had experienced the isolation, burnout, and spirit-
destroying consequences of the traditional hierarchical leadership
model. I once heard myself describing to a clergy colleague my
sense of ministry as struggling to keep my head above water in
the swirling, shifting currents of the church while the people
of the church stood on the shoreline watching to see if I would
make it. My friend said, "That's right, so get used to it." I left
that conversation thinking, "If that is the truth, then there is
something terribly wrong with the model." Listening to other
pastors, I have heard them express the same sense of isolation
and exhausting struggle. When, out of spiritual desperation, I
began a daily practice of sitting in stillness with God, I discerned
over time another more life-giving path.

In deep communion with God's Spirit I experienced the reality of an empowering, profoundly mutual, liberating relationship free from the grasping, possessive, competitive, fearful, and self-protective strivings that are so much a part of our contemporary culture. The Holy Love that embraced me in the stillness of contemplative prayer invited me to express this same companionship in all my relations and it accompanied me as I sought to live my prayer. As I was drawn into intimacy with God's heart, I discovered that I experienced a growing dissonance with the conventional wisdom and practice of "top-down" pastoral leadership. The image of being alone in the torrent of church and culture was challenged by what the Spirit revealed to me in prayer. The call of CBC and the promise of Marcia's companionship were the grace I needed to trust the Spirit's leading.

Although there is some truth to the statement that Marcia and I created this leadership model at Central, it is just as true to say that it created us. The partnership model that we received and nurtured emerged from the communion of Central Baptist Church. It is an expression of the creative, iconoclastic spirit of our congregation. The people of Central Baptist Church have a healthy distrust of the values and structures of our consumer-oriented society. The life and spirit of Jesus, who challenged the imperial powers and stood conventional wisdom on its head, guides and nourishes our communal path. And so it was into fertile soil that the seed of a new pastoral model was planted. The Jesus-life embodied in CBC's communion met the desire that Marcia and I brought for a new, more inclusive and mutual leadership style. God formed this mix of "mud and clay" into pastoral partnership, breathing into it the breath of God's life.

But the partnership model of pastoral leadership created us in an even more important way. When CBC, Marcia, and I began this adventure none of us knew what the path ahead would bring. Like Abraham and Sarah we set out not knowing where we were going. One of the first dialogue sermons Marcia and I preached together included a reading of Dr. Seuss's book,

Oh, the Places You'll Go. It was our attempt to signal that we did not have partnership mapped out, nor did we have a clear understanding of our destination. We were convinced that we were being called and led toward something new, but we did not have a clue how to get there or even where "there" was.

The consciousness that our path was one of continuing discernment was one of the early gifts of learning that we received. We discovered that we were being invited by the experience of partnership to embrace in trust an attitude of "not knowing." Having been trained and acculturated in the normalcy of hierarchical leadership, we found ourselves struggling between accepting this invitation to trust and maintaining our own internalized expectations, preconceptions, and control needs. This struggle continued over the eleven years we ministered together, and it is where we experienced the greatest gifts of self-discovery and spiritual growth. Partnership transformed us as persons and pastors.

The pastoral partnership model that Marcia and I evolved was fun, life-giving, and creative. It established a foundation on which the current pastoral team at CBC is building. I am very grateful to have had the opportunity to share ministry with Marcia at CBC, and I am profoundly thankful that she has written about our experiences and learnings as pastoral partners. I pray that through this book other pastoral teams will be encouraged and strengthened in their ministries and new teams will be inspired to trust the Spirit's leading toward another way—a path of new spiritual community.

Marcus Pomeroy

Preface

∞I would like to say that I began to imagine partnership—nonhierarchical leadership, with shared vision, power, and responsibility—the moment I began my pastoral ministry in 1986. But that is not true. At the time, I looked at the clergy around me, including my mentors, and began to replicate the model that I saw—the pastor as leader extraordinaire, empowered by education, authority, position, and resources. The assumption was that this kind of pastor was most keenly in touch with all things spiritual and most likely to know, understand, and reflect the heart and mind of God. My head said, "This is how it's done. This is what you were trained to be and do." My gut said, "This isn't me. There has got to be another way."

I experienced my dis-ease with traditional pastoral ministry on several levels. In the mid-1980s, I was one of few women pastors in a large metropolitan area, even though my denomination had been ordaining women for more than one hundred years. Every time I attended a clergy gathering, I felt like an intruder in the male locker room, where stories and struggles were shared around me but not with or even by me. The influence of patriarchy—the assumption that males are entitled to position and power—was strong, as was the hierarchy that accompanied it.

These pastors wrestled with the perceived need to have the answers, be in charge, move to bigger and bigger churches; I was not a part of that conversation, nor did I want to be.

I also was not convinced these were values that reflected either the rapidly changing culture or Jesus, for that matter. The postmodern shift was already well underway, whether anyone could name it or not, and it was apparent to me that, as leaders in the church, we needed to create new models for ministry to respond to what was emerging around us.

In conjunction with all of this, I began to look again at Jesus—the leader he was, the ministry he lived, and the model he presented. I did not see his leadership style reflected in the patriarchal, hierarchical push around me. This realization began to give me greater courage to listen to myself and to the Spirit for the inklings of another way.

So began my desire to live into a model for ministry that empowered each person, as Jesus did, to be both transformed and a transformer in the world. When I looked at Jesus, I saw a model for ministry that was widely inclusive, delegated power, shared authority, and thrived with the multiplication of gifts. It was ministry that expanded as the lives touched by it grew, a ministry that took seriously the reordering of power in community and in the world. I longed for this kind of ministry and for the opportunity to give flesh to the invitation I felt rising in my spirit, an invitation to dismantle the traditional power and authority structures we find inherent in every local congregation and to incarnate Jesus's example in a fresh new way.

That opportunity came when I was called to Central Baptist Church of Wayne, Pennsylvania. There I was joined by my colleague, Rev. Dr. Marcus Pomeroy, a pilgrim whose experience, although very different from mine, led him in this same direction and whose heart burned with this same fire. Together, over 10 years of shared ministry, we lived into a vision of ministry that, as a pastoral team and with our congregation, we called partnership. This book is about the unfolding of that partnership—how we defined it and how we came to live it—as pastoral partners and with the Central Baptist congregation.

As we lived into this new way of being, we began to notice several things. We discovered that very little had been written about practicing the model we envisioned. Partnership had been described by some but mostly in theoretical language; it had been an idea, not an experience. We found ourselves not only writing our own definition but also creating our own map, trusting our own instincts, making our own mistakes. These, as well as trusted collaborators and the Spirit, became our guides. These influences turned out to be a powerful combination! Along the way, we began to be encouraged by others who watched, asked questions, and invited us to partner with them as they developed new models of their own. This book is one way we hope to return that encouragement—by sharing with pastors, leaders, congregations, and seminarians the invitation to listen closely to God's voice, to follow intently the Spirit's movement, and to know that it is not only possible but a joyful, life-giving experience to live a vision of God's reign that shapes and suits your ministry.

In light of Jesus's radical life and ministry, I believe that the church needs to make drastic changes if we are to take seriously our call to embody the gospel in the world. For centuries, the church embraced hierarchy, patriarchy, and a host of other oppressive constructs; Jesus's message has been reduced from one that confronts and transforms to one that conforms and perpetuates restrictive tradition. Partnership and its resultant deepening of spiritual community moves us one step closer to living God's reign. Partnership invites us on a journey that has the power to transform us as leaders (clergy and nonclergy alike), as human beings, and as the church. It is challenging and exciting, and it requires hard work. It is also energizing, engaging, and empowering. Partnership unleashes the Spirit in a fresh way to create a new vision and reality among us.

Acknowledgments

When talking about partnership, clearly my desire is to express my gratitude to the many people who have participated and labored in this vision. I want to thank and celebrate the people of Central Baptist Church, Wayne, Pennsylvania, who with hope and expectation first allowed and then encouraged this vision to come to life within them. This dynamic community of faith entered into this vision with all its heart and became a transforming force as it embraced the life that began to rise from within. They continue to live the vision as a congregation, discerning the changes to heart, mind, spirit, and structure again and again, that they might more fully reflect God's reign.

I am grateful for the community of mentors, educators, and friends who have accompanied me on this journey over the years and who have repeatedly urged me to "write the vision; make it plain" (Habakkuk 2:2) so that others might follow in the way. I am thankful also to those who sought Marcus and I out in their own longing for fresh models for ministry; their interest and inquiry always helped us to clarify what we were doing and encouraged us to continue.

I am grateful to the Alban Institute for this opportunity and especially for Kristy Pullen, whose passion for collaborative ministry is exemplified in her own ministry. As a gifted leader, Kristy participated in the emergence of partnership at Central Baptist, and her wise counsel and ardent support was important for both pastors and congregation alike. Beth Gaede has been an encouraging and gifted editor whose confidence, guidance, and expertise are deeply appreciated.

My deep love and gratitude goes to my family—my husband, Rich, and children Sarah, Adam, and Thomas. You are always supportive, encouraging, and proud, and that has been an incredible blessing to me.

The names and faces of so many more of you emerge before my eyes. Life is not a solitary journey but a collaborative celebration and expression of God's love and grace. Thank you for the gift of your presence, now and always. My hope is that we will all grow into true partnership in the likeness of Jesus.

Most of all I want to thank Marcus Pomeroy, my pastoral colleague for a decade, who heard the Holy's voice and urging and who envisioned, struggled, laughed, cried, and boldly lived this new reality alongside me. This writing is infused with his spirit as well as mine; in partnership, such commingling multiplies the gifts and enriches the endeavor.

As I write these pages, my ministry at Central Baptist with Marcus has come to an end and a new call to teach has begun. My deepest hope is that an increasing number of leaders will catch their own glimpse of the transformative vision of God's reign and dare to move toward prophetic models for life and ministry.

1 ⌒

Imagining
Alternatives

⌒Most of us hoping to build something new would ideally begin with a clear space, new materials, the necessary resources, and a well thought-out plan. When committing ourselves to embodying a new leadership style we called partnership, my colleague and I, however, could not simply erase the reality of church tradition or our own life experience. We had to begin with who and what was already there, using our vision and gifts to dismantle old structures, reinterpret assumptions, and imagine new ways of relating as leaders and as the faith community together. We began by envisioning what the church would look like if it embraced nonhierarchy—that is, if it let go of the historical need to rank and order, to limit power and authority, to separate by gender and privilege. We began to imagine what challenging hierarchy and reordering relationships in the local church could mean. We began by acknowledging that the pull of the past and its influence on how all of us act in the present is powerful and persuasive.

Partnership, as Marcus and I defined and lived it, is a freely chosen, nonhierarchical relationship of mutual vision, power, and responsibility with equal commitments, risks, and rewards for the purpose of birthing new spiritual community. It is a radical way of leading that reflects Jesus's own ministry—that is, his reordering of power, assumptions, and expectations—in order to bring new life, to deepen spiritual community, and to open the community to God's transforming Spirit.

While *partnership* is a common word, we have defined it with a very specific meaning. We have come to use it to describe our hope for *relationships built on mutuality, vision, and trust.* Partnership in ministry invites us to share our gifts and passion, our visions and hope. This collaboration leads us to a fuller recognition of God among us, a deeper understanding of God between us, a more authentic discernment of God's call within us, and a more holistic embodiment of God because of us. Partnership is an organic expression of leadership and community within and among God's people.

To successfully create a new kind of pastoral relationship, we would need to resist the norms and patterns that held us and the church in an oppressive, unimaginative place. We would need to be intentional. We would need to hold the vision constantly before us. We would need to embody what others could hardly begin to think about. We would need to demonstrate by our words and our actions what nonhierarchical relationship is all about.

Leadership is a popular subject of conversation and writing in the church today; perhaps this says something about the desire to look freshly at the leadership styles the church has assumed over the years and to imagine what leadership style will be life giving for the years to come. As we in the church think about a new model for leadership, it is important to know where this book begins.

A leader is one who has been called to use gifts, talents, educational preparation, and energies for particular functions, at a particular time, in a particular community. Leaders are vested with authority given to them by the community. How leaders characterize the authority given to them and how they use the power that goes with that authority is central to partnership.

Partnership views leadership as cooperative and communal, in mutual relationship with other leaders and with the congregation, and by sharing power with other leaders and the congregation. While they are indeed called to be leaders, the power they share is asymmetrical, rather than hierarchical. Asymmetrical power acknowledges that leaders may have roles, functions, even access to information different from other leaders or congregants. Leaders do not use power or roles to set themselves above or against other leaders or the congregation; rather, they consider these resources for working with the congregation to deepen its spiritual and communal life. In partnership Marcus and I talked about relationships as an interconnecting web; asymmetrical power is demonstrated as energy moves in and through the web. This energy is the Holy Spirit's gift; as the Spirit moves and people respond to its direction in a specific way, the focus of the web shifts toward that energy. Leaders may emerge at any time and any place. Partnership invites leaders and followers together to create a new spiritual community. More will be said about this, along with mutuality, power, and the web in later chapters.

Partnership Story

"I'd like to introduce you to my partner in ministry," Marcus began, motioning a friend in my direction. "Oh, how nice to meet you," she offered with a smile, coming forward to take my hand. "You must be Marcus's associate." Shocked and frustrated that it happened again, Marcus shot back, "No! She's *not* my associate. She's my partner." Obviously confused, she looked from me to him and back again, replying weakly, "Oh yeah, sure. That's what I meant."

The "it" that happened "again" is the assumption of hierarchy, the assumption that when a man and a woman work together, the man must hold a dominant position in relationship to the woman—that a rank and an order to the relationship are necessary. It is a common, if dangerous, assumption. The assumption is common in that hierarchy is, and long has been, the normative relationship between women and men in society and in the church. The assumption is dangerous because it is accompanied by predictable expectations, behaviors, and responses. For example, in the encounter described above, the assumption is that the male is primary and the female "other" in relationship. Hierarchy makes many assumptions—assumptions that the church and the world have chosen to embrace, in spite of Jesus's prophetic reordering of relationships. Resisting the hierarchy of his own time, Jesus carefully and creatively invites his followers to see themselves and each other in a new light. He opens up space for God's Spirit to work in ways that offer us fresh alternatives and invites us to something new.

Miracle by Relationship

The apostles came back to Jesus and reported all that they had done and taught. Jesus said to them, "Come away by yourselves to someplace more remote, and rest awhile." For there were many people coming and going, and the apostles hadn't had time to eat. So they went away in a boat to a deserted area.

The people saw them leaving and many recognized them, so they ran together on foot from all the cities and got there ahead of the apostles. When Jesus went ashore, there was a large crowd waiting for him, and he felt compassion for them because they were like sheep without a shepherd. So he began to teach them many things.

By now it was getting very late, and his disciples came up to him and said, "This is a deserted place and it's very late. Why not dismiss them so they can go to the nearby farms and villages and buy something to eat?"

Jesus replied, "Give them something to eat yourselves."
They answered, "You want us to spend half a year's wages
on bread for them to eat?"

"How many loaves do you have?" Jesus asked. "Go
look."

When they found out they reported back, "Five, and two
fish."

Jesus told them to have the people sit down on the grass
in groups of hundreds and fifties. Then Jesus took the five
loaves and the two fish, raised his eyes to heaven and said
the blessing. Jesus broke the loaves and handed them to the
disciples to distribute among the people. He also passed out
the two fish among them.

They all ate until they had their fill. The disciples gathered
up the leftovers and filled twelve baskets of broken bread and
fish. In all, five thousand families ate that day.

Mark 6:30–44

Jesus's miraculous feeding of the multitude is recorded in
all four Gospel accounts. Biblical scholars have viewed it as a
miracle demonstrating God's power to provide for humanity's
needs. With Jesus's words of blessing, a finite amount of bread
and fish is transformed into an ample supply of nourishment
for a hungry crowd. The disciples are puzzled participants. The
recipients are passive observers. All are astonished that there are
leftovers. In a unique display of power, Jesus reveals his divine
position at the hierarchy's apex with everything and everyone
at his command.

There is, however, another way to view this text as pointed
out by Susan Willhauck and Jacqulyn Thorpe in *The Web of
Women's Leadership: Recasting Congregational Ministry.*[1] Citing
Parker Palmer, they suggest that rather than showing Jesus's
domination the miracle reveals Jesus's invitation to a new expression of relationship, what Marcus and I called partnership—that
is, an opportunity to become participants in God's transforming nature. I find this event one of the most dramatic examples

of Jesus modeling nonhierarchical leadership and relationship in the Gospel accounts. If we can begin to imagine ourselves in the text—in this case, sitting on the grass listening to Jesus amid the crowd, looking at the faces around us, noticing our own hunger—we can begin to catch a glimpse of God's Spirit at work both then in the crowd and now in us. Jesus invites both the disciples and the gathered crowd to participate in something truly miraculous—the abundance of gifts and resources that emerges when we offer ourselves in mutuality to each other.

Jesus begins by inviting the disciples to become partners with him in addressing the crowd's needs. Instead of sending the crowd away, Jesus suggests a way that the need for food could be met then and there with the resources that were available to the entire group. Rather than acting unilaterally to solve the problem, Jesus enlists the disciples' participation by helping them to see the possibilities that exist among them. After assessing what is available, Jesus instructs the disciples to organize the crowd into manageable groups. As happens with most of us when we find ourselves in a crowd that is organized into small groupings, I imagine that these folks, when gathered face to face, might no longer seem like strangers to one another but could begin to recognize each other as followers of Jesus and learners together. I also imagine that it was unlikely, in their context, for them to go off for the day unprepared to care for their own need to eat. As they encounter each other as new but hungry friends, they begin to share what they have with each other. The crowd distributes the loaves and fish that have been blessed, and there is more than enough to go around!

These two very different interpretations naturally raise the question: what then was the actual miracle? Was it that Jesus could by some divine power multiply the five loaves and the two fish into limitless supply? This traditional interpretation certainly complies with a hierarchical perspective. Having the ability to control the situation, Jesus uses power over the group to supply their need; they become passive recipients of divine grace. But the second interpretation suggests that the miracle might be something else. The miracle in the second interpretation is the transformation of hierarchy to nonhierarchy, of unilateral action to sharing, of individualism to mutuality in relationship—to partnership. Men, women, and children see each other's need as their own and, following Jesus's example, give from the abundance of shared resources, so the result is not only substantial, but the people actually have more than enough to go around. The miracle, then, is not Jesus's use of divine power over the situation but Jesus's use of shared power, which all of us can embody, to release the gifts already present.

Hierarchy, with structures that prescribe, restricts the movement of power and Spirit. Its predictability leaves little space for spontaneity, for possibility, or for the transformative nature of God's Spirit. Dismantling hierarchy opens up opportunities for God's Spirit to work within and among us. In this new space, individuals are encouraged to claim and act out of power that is rightfully their own. Those who doubt that the second interpretation qualifies as a miracle might consider an example from our own times. We know that the earth produces enough food and clean water to satisfy the needs of all, yet people starve; the problem lies in distribution and pollution. Certainly it would be miraculous if children, women, and men today could look each other in the face, recognize a common humanity, and offer the resources each has available, so that the entire world might not only have enough but also thrive and flourish. Jesus reorders relationships so that all might share the power of God's Spirit.

The Assumptions of Hierarchy

First, to identify and dismantle hierarchy to make opportunity for nonhierarchy, understanding the nature of hierarchy is important. Those who ascribe to hierarchy make many assumptions about authority and power. One of the first assumptions is that hierarchy not only describes "the way things are" but that hierarchy is, in fact, the way *God* intended things to be. Yet the study of Scripture reveals an invitation to be in relationships that are mutual, respectful, and life giving. From the creation accounts in Genesis that instruct human beings to look after the earth in responsible stewardship (not to rule over it or each other) to the Christian community's early beginnings when women and men shared leadership, hierarchy has not been the divinely ordered mandate, even if for centuries we have acted as if it is. In addition to the assumption that hierarchy is the normative way of relating in the world, hierarchy by definition makes its own assumptions about power, gender, and privilege, all of which partnership actively resists.

The first assumption hierarchy makes is that power is limited, that it is finite. Because a defined amount of power is available, obtaining and holding onto power become the ultimate goal. In hierarchy, people's perception that power is scarce results in their spending energy devising ways to take illegitimate power—power that is not their own—and to protect power, so that others will not have access to it.

Viewed as limited and scarce, power gives hierarchy its shape, a pyramid in which the majority of people reside on or near the bottom while a few rise to the top. Power is amassed at the pyramid's apex, resulting in the least possible number of people—perhaps just one, the leader—having the greatest amount of power. Movement from the bottom of the pyramid to the top requires gaining power at others' expense. The only way to acquire power is to take it. The only way to keep power is to use it to control others.

Value is assigned to those who have access to power: the greater access, the greater the power, and the greater the person's value; the lesser access to power, the less the person's power and value. Power itself is the end goal. As a result, hierarchy orders and ranks individuals and assigns them value based on their potential or achieved power.

This insistence on ranking is reflected in the word *hierarchy* and is embodied, among other places, in the church. Look up "hierarchy" in any dictionary, and you will find a definition that links it to the church. While the early church had no formal ranking in its leadership, such models arose by the third century as the church took on more formal structure, moving from the private domain of house churches (and shared female and male leadership) to the public domain (and male leadership). What became normative in church leadership was more a reflection of the secular empire in which the church resided than a reflection of the shared community Jesus envisioned.

A second assumption of hierarchy is that one gender is dominant over another. In our society and in the church the male assumes supremacy over the female. Power, authority, value, and privilege are assigned to men, leaving women to occupy the lower portion of the hierarchical pyramid with few or none of these resources or the possibility to obtain them. The few women who do rise within hierarchy's structure must do so within the confines of its assumptions, embracing its values and playing the game by its self-serving rules. As a result, most women do not experience themselves as valued by the hierarchical system and are forced to accept the limitations hierarchy places on them as individuals, as well as on their talents and gifts. This restriction has been particularly tragic for the church.

Hierarchy's gender preference has limited the expression of women's voices and gifts in the church. Even at this time, women continue to struggle to find acceptance and receive calls to leadership in the church. Women liberated by Jesus to reclaim their divinely intended partnership relationships with men continue to be remarginalized as hierarchy forces them to the edges. In this reality, women, men, and the church all suffer significant loss.

In addition to the first two assumptions—one that hierarchy simply reflects how the world is and the other that power is limited and patriarchy is normative—hierarchy assumes privilege. Hierarchy supposes the right to define what is normative and acceptable to society. As a result, hierarchy makes decisions about inclusion based on race, sexual orientation, economic standing, and societal status. Against these norms all other norms are judged. Unfortunately, the church has affirmed this standard; it is reflected, for example, in decisions about who is an acceptable candidate for ordination and leadership. Once again, hierarchy establishes a system of value and rank, rewarding those who fit its ideal with access and power.

Some have said that hierarchy is "the air we breathe." While its pervasiveness indeed makes it so, many of us who envision an alternative find ourselves having trouble choosing between breathing or not breathing at all. If nonhierarchical relationships were the intention at creation and were in fact normative in early history, then Jesus's actions and words take on added importance as we consider whether he supported the assumption of hierarchy or actively sought to undermine and subvert the hierarchical system and replace it with something else. Both biblical and cultural evidence suggest that hierarchy is neither the only way nor the ideal way for women and men to live in relationship.

Jesus introduces a reordering of relationships, a nonhierarchical means of relating that denies hierarchy's assumptions. Power, gender, and privilege are reinterpreted in light of God's reign rather than the reign of men. Partnership dares to do just that; it dares to remember that hierarchy has not always been the air we breathe, nor was it God's intention in creation. A construct of humanity, hierarchy and its assumptions must be critiqued by the liberating action of the Christ, and alternate relationship models must be brought to light again. Partnership is one such expression as mutuality in relationship is brought to life.

Assumptions of Nonhierarchy

Partnership is born out of a desire to build relationships and to offer leadership outside hierarchy's tenacious grip. Opening up space for other means of relating requires the dismantling of hierarchy. Partnership is not intended as another way to operate alongside hierarchy; rather, it is an intentional effort to expose the oppression within hierarchy, to dismantle its structure, and to create an entirely new way of being in relationship. As a result, Marcus and I used the language of "nonhierarchy"—a whole set of words indicating that what we are speaking about is *not* hierarchy. Partnership envisions a web of mutual relationships that are life giving. Just as hierarchy carries assumptions about power, gender, and privilege, nonhierarchy has its own assumptions and offers a liberating perspective on how people relate to one another.

Power Is Limitless

The first assumption of nonhierarchy is that power is limitless; there is an infinite supply. Nonhierarchy believes that each individual has power that can be used to benefit self and others and that this power is intended to be shared. Shared power is abundant, nonrestrictive, free flowing, generous. Like the loaves and the fish, shared power grows beyond expectation. Nonhierarchy discovers that power shared is power multiplied; that is, the more power is used in mutuality to benefit all, the more power emerges from within the group. Power is not to be hoarded but to be offered for the well-being of all. In this way, nonhierarchy evokes shared power from others and the entire relationship-web benefits.

Unlike hierarchy whose structure is pyramidal, nonhierarchy is best reflected in the image of an interconnecting web. Multidimensional, multidirectional, and inclusive, this web connects individuals and groups with each other so that power and resources, energy and insight might benefit all. As a result, anyone who shares nonhierarchy's values is welcomed to participate, not to compete but to cooperate, not to limit but to expand. This intentional sharing of power dismantles a hierarchal structure and invites people to participate in an organic relationship network that encourages, empowers, and gives life to all.

Inclusivity Is Valued

A second assumption of nonhierarchy is that both women and men are equally talented and capable, equally able to participate mutually in relationships and leadership. Nonhierarchy recognizes the contribution that all humanity potentially makes within the web and celebrates the strengths and gifts each of us discovers as we claim our right to be whole persons. Patriarchy or matriarchy has no place within nonhierarchy because mutual respect and equality are shared by all.

Nonhierarchy discards the pretense of privilege and instead values the full inclusion of all. For nonhierarchy, distinctiveness among the community serves to strengthen the whole and diversity adds wisdom and insight. The web of relationships expands as more people come to embrace it, considering each participant a valued and important part. As a result of inclusion, the web reflects the depth of resources that results when people bring all of their gifts to serve a common purpose.

What Nonhierarchy Looked Like in One Partnership

When my partner in ministry, Marcus, and I began conversations about the possibility of working together, we were each clear about one thing: neither of us had any interest in a hierarchical relationship. What we were not too sure of, however, was how a nonhierarchical relationship would look in a congregational setting.

Sunday morning worship is the only time the majority of the Central Baptist congregation would come together in a given week, so we concluded that nonhierarchy had to be clearly demonstrated during the worship experience. For us, this meant sharing equally the responsibility for preaching and the celebration of baptism and communion. We agreed that we needed to visibly demonstrate nonhierarchy in worship, not only between us as pastoral staff, but also in our relationship with the congregation. Although congregation members had served as worship leaders alongside the congregation's previous pastors and sometimes had preached, we worked to increase sharing this leadership. Likewise, many gifted volunteer musicians share their talents on any given Sunday, alongside the choir members and the professional musicians who direct the congregation's music ministry. Each worship leader and musician alike sits in the pews among the congregation and moves to the appropriate location to lead. In this way leaders model the belief that people are called out of the community to offer their gifts rather than to claim seats of position or power. Nonhierarchy gives expression to the web of relationships that make up our faith community and to the Spirit's movement throughout that web for the benefit of all.

Other dimensions of our ministry expressed nonhierarchy as well. While some pastoral leaders may assume the role and responsibilities of a CEO, claiming final authority and power over decision making, for example, we have instead viewed our role as nurturers of spiritual discovery and growth and as encouragers of communal life. While we had responsibility for some day-to-day decisions, we preferred to serve as resource people for elected boards and for ministry and ad hoc groups by providing them with input and information they request, making their own decisions with our support. As a congregation, we shared information and access to the decision-making process and sought to gain consensus before moving in a new or different direction. As a result, opportunity is built in for all to have a chance to express themselves, either through elected board members or by direct input.

Nonhierarchy is demonstrated in simple but significant ways through the language all of us use. Staff are listed in the bulletin alphabetically in groups according to their ministry specialization. Marcus and I referred to ourselves as "one of the pastors at Central Baptist Church," not "the pastor." When others referred to one of us as "the pastor," we carefully made the correction. Although the congregation reflects a high level of educational expertise, we did not use titles (Rev. or Dr.) in speech or in printed materials when referring to each other, either as pastors or as congregants. We preferred to be simply "Marcia" and "Marcus," "Jan" or "Bud," reducing the tendency to assign power or status to some and not others. Few, if any, adults are even referred to within the congregation as "Mr.," "Mrs.," "Miss," or "Ms." Everyone is called by her or his first name, adults as well as children. This too reflects relationships that are nonhierarchical, in this case in relationship to age.

Working and living in relationships that are collaborative, noncompetitive, and nonhierarchical in a hierarchical culture is challenging but not impossible. It takes constant vigilance to be aware of the "air we breathe" and to resist the assumptions that surround us. Marcus and I found that we must always be attentive to the dynamic at work around and between us, a way of relating that is sometimes a result of cultural assumptions, sometimes the result of those who consciously or unconsciously threaten to subvert our work, or sometimes even as a result of our own carelessness as we reverted to habits and patterns, reminding us that we too are hierarchy's products.

The Invitation

Partnership invites us to take seriously the cultural construct of hierarchy, its assumptions and implications, and to place those alongside Jesus's model of transformative leadership. The Greco-Roman culture of Jesus's day, and even later expressions of the Christian church, embodied hierarchy and its assumptions about power, gender, and privilege. Jesus and the immediate postresurrection faith community, however, demonstrate relationships that value shared power, appreciate diversity, and provide equal access to leadership and authority and participation for all. Partnership seeks to dismantle hierarchy's oppression by reordering community with an understanding and an appreciation for weblike relationships and the contributions of all.

Nonhierarchical leadership seeks to imitate Jesus's own style as he invited the disciples and all who gathered around him to become equal participants in God's unfolding reign. The feeding of the more than five thousand illustrates the abundance of gifts revealed when available power and resources are shared among us. Jesus chooses to lead in this way so that his followers might embody his nonhierarchical vision in our relationships with one another. Such an invitation is a direct challenge not only to our culture but also to the institutional church in most of its forms today. Partnership calls us to leading and being the community of faith in a new way. It relies not on the way things are but on faith communities' vision and courage to make real the way God invites us to be.

2 ⌒

The Gift of
Interdependence

⌒**W**hen congregations and their leaders move from hierarchy to nonhierarchy, we discover ourselves focusing less on ourselves as individuals and more on ourselves as people in relationship. Mutuality describes the nature of a partnership relationship; it frames how we act and think about vision, power, and responsibility. Mutuality invites a level playing field, sharing, and deep respect. Each participant is valued equally, and each person's contributions benefit all.

A Partnership Story

A typical morning at Central Baptist may have started like this: one of us walked into the other's office and began, "We need to make a list."

"OK," came the response. "List away!"

"Well, we need to organize a potential/new members' dinner, so we should gather those names. That means phone calls of invitation. Whose turn is it to host, yours or mine?"

"Mine," was the reply. "You hosted last time. We also have to work on worship plans for the next series and go over the Cabinet agenda. What else?"

"I have an update from the Board of Outreach meeting last night."

"And I have one from the Board of Communal Life. Oh. And I had an idea for the Salvador Partners Mission Group luncheon, but I need some help."

"OK. Put it on the list."

And so it went. Back and forth—sharing information, ideas, and responsibilities. This is mutuality in partnership: ministry in all its aspects is shared and owned for better or worse by both partners. It is not "my board" and "your board," my problem or yours, but ours—ours to work at together; ours to envision, implement, struggle with, even resist. ("But I wrote the front page of the newsletter last time; it's your turn.") Each of us brought particular gifts, talents, experience, biases, likes, and dislikes to the conversation. All of it got mixed together. What started as "mine" or "yours" was transformed into "ours." New energy, new insight, new possibilities were born. It happened when two of us worked together. It happened in small groups and even within the congregation as a whole. Mutuality happens when we view ourselves as interconnected with others, when our joys and concerns are honestly, authentically owned and shared.

Mutuality resists everything our culture teaches us about being independent and competitive. In place of "do it yourself," mutuality invites us to vulnerability and openness to our need for others; independence is replaced by interdependence. Instead of the self-focused notion "I can do it better," mutuality, and its invitation to collaboration, gives life to concepts and resources that emerge out of community, things not imagined by individuals working alone. Mutuality invites us into shared ministry where gifts are multiplied and struggles shared in service to one another and to Christ.

Mutuality describes the nature of relationships in partnership and is central to how Jesus related to those around him. Mutuality frames how we think about power, vision, and responsibility.

It inverts hierarchical systems, welcomes diversity, and searches for opportunities for interconnectedness nurtured in weblike relationships. How we embody mutuality in ministry begins with the model we have in Jesus.

A New Paradigm

> Another dispute arose among them about who would be regarded as the greatest. But Jesus said to them, "Earthly rulers domineer over their people. Those who exercise authority over them are called their 'benefactors.' This must not happen with you. Let the greatest among you be like the youngest. Let the leader among you become the follower. For who is the greater? The one who reclines at a meal, or the one who serves it? Isn't it the one reclining at table? Yet I am here among you as the one who serves you."
>
> Luke 22:24–27

The disciples' conversation around the table is not unlike that overheard on any elementary school playground or acted out in any corporate boardroom. It reflects an assumption of hierarchy and a valuing of individualism. Each person operates alone. Competition is the name of the game. Someone, and only one, must be considered "the greatest." The disciples are reminded that this exchange expresses cultural and societal values then even as now. It reflects how the civil authorities and power brokers operate. Jesus, however, envisions something radically different. Jesus suggests that, rather than striving to be at the top of the heap, people who want to be considered great should actually be like the people customarily considered the least—children and servants, neither of whom had status or opportunity in biblical times. In just a few short sentences, the hierarchy is dismantled. It is not what we can achieve that makes us great but who we are in relationship to one another.

Jesus proposes mutuality by suggesting grown adults should become like children and free people like servants. Apparently he sees something in both children and servants that more clearly reflects the realm of God. Consider a child: dependent, wholly in need of others for nurture and encouragement in growth and learning. Intuitively, children reach out to those around them for sustenance and support. They unashamedly need others. Similarly, a person is a servant in relationship to someone or something (like an institution such as the church); one cannot be a servant in isolation. Jesus's vision for the disciples and for us is not that we compete to outdo one another, valuing individualism (prioritizing self-interest over the interest of the group) and establishing hierarchy, but rather that we seek to be in life-giving relationship to each other. A child must be in relationship to someone else to flourish. A servant cannot be a servant without someone to serve. People are not meant to be isolated, competitive, and alone. We are created to be in relationship— relationships that allow us to share our vulnerabilities and resources for everyone's benefit.

Jesus's invitation to take on the servant role makes many people uncomfortable, especially women. No one desires to be taken advantage of, to be defined only by the tasks they perform for others, to live without freedom and opportunity. Hierarchy and patriarchy have created experiences of second-class citizenry—servanthood—for many people, particularly women, people of color, and sexual-orientation minorities. But this is not Jesus's vision. Jesus invites us to be in life-giving relationships; he encourages us to be as he was, "among you as one who serves" (Luke 22:27).

To be "among you" is to be in a relationship of mutuality, to attend to each other's needs and to support each other's growth, not so that one may outrank another but so that all are supported and nurtured. Jesus invites the disciples—and us—into a relationship that levels the hierarchy and deepens our communion with one other. Jesus models this mutuality by becoming the servant in the disciples' midst, shattering their expectations and inviting them to rethink their assumptions about greatness. Followers are invited by Jesus to relationships of mutuality where the world's values are dramatically transformed by the values of God's reign. In this passage Jesus reveals the limited, dysfunctional nature of present systems and dramatically demonstrates another way of being in relationship with one another.

Mutuality: Partnership's True Nature

The true nature of partnership is *mutuality,* a word that characterizes how partners think, act, and live together. Resisting the idea that we are isolated and independent, mutuality insists that we envision ourselves always in relationship to another, a partnership built on shared vision, power, and responsibility. Mutuality can occur when two or more people commit themselves to such a relationship; it can also happen in a larger group when a spirit of consensus building and cooperation becomes the norm.

Mutuality in relationship creates several positive dynamics:

- Mutuality dismantles hierarchy
- Mutuality invites diversity.
- Mutuality creates a web of relationships.

By dismantling hierarchy, mutuality offers a corrective to the societal norm. By its very nature, hierarchy pits people against each other, increasing suspicion and anxiety in relationship. Mutuality, on the other hand, links us to each other in a positive way by strengthening ties, revealing uniqueness, and encouraging potential in a way that mirrors the creative goodness of creation itself. Marcus and I discovered that mutuality allowed each of us to bring the richness of our strengths to the partnership without competition; likewise, we could reveal our weaknesses or struggles without feeling diminished.

When people experience themselves as valued and respected, when their ideas, gifts, vision, and personhood are affirmed, they become willing to be more open and honest with one another and themselves. This openness is possible because mutuality evokes trust between us. In trusting one another, we can become vulnerable, revealing more of our true selves, and deepen our relationships with each other. Knowing that someone will hold my joys and struggles in trust opens up safe space where I can discover myself and God. I found this true between Marcus and me as well as in the small covenantal groups that formed and met within our larger congregation. Mutuality invites us to deeper, more meaningful relationships.

Mutuality invites diversity. It welcomes a broad assortment of people and possibilities together to discover the richness that creation affords. Everyone is welcome; everyone contributes. Marcus and I have talked about mutuality as a messy interaction of interdependent systems, a gathering of diverse people and groups committed to community, all of whom share a common vision and desire to improve and to transform. Mutuality is creative risk-taking that is not afraid to make errors. New ideas are tried; some succeed and some fail. New interpretations of life and faith are offered; some are received with enthusiasm and some offend. This messiness is achieved only through diversity, when a multiplicity of gifts, visions, and insights are gathered to deepen and broaden the experience of all. Mutuality values such diversity, finding it a necessary ingredient in relationships as we seek to reflect God's creativity. Not threatened by a variety of experiences and opinions, mutuality celebrates diversity as a means of growth. Each partner brings to mutual relationship gifts, insights, and experiences that are his or hers alone. Mutuality welcomes each one, recognizing that this broad spectrum serves to stimulate and to inform, to challenge and to create. The congregation of Central Baptist, Marcus, and I valued boards, committees, and ad hoc groups that represented the variety of

theology, age, gender, sexual orientation, racial/ethnic back-
ground, and life experience represented within our congregation.
Rather than viewing diversity as a potential for divisiveness, we
saw it as a reflection of the creative expression of God's reign.

Mutuality creates a relationship web where more mutuality
flourishes and grows. As people experience themselves connected
to one another, they become committed to freedom, respect,
creativity, and shared ownership. Mutuality focuses not on the
individual but on the relationship with another. It requires
letting go of individual ego needs in return for the increased
growth of interior freedom—freedom to grow and to try and
to do within the community's nurture and support. The web is
the interwoven network of these caring relationships that seek
to nurture and encourage the best in one another. When you
imagine the web, think not of a spider's neat, circular web but
of endless, interweaving connections that crisscross each other
in myriad ways. In such a web, there is not one central focus
but many. Connections reach across, under, over, even through
one another, keeping those on the outside in relationship with
those toward the middle. Changes in leadership naturally occur
within the web as the group and its needs evolve, as new webs
emerge, and as mutuality invites all to participate. Mutuality's
desire for interrelatedness extends the web of relationships while
keeping us connected to one another.

What Mutuality in One Partnership
Looked Like

In the definition of partnership (a freely chosen, nonhierarchical
relationship of mutual vision, power, and responsibility with
equal commitments, risks, and rewards for the purpose of birthing new spiritual community), the word *mutual* modifies three
things: vision, power, and responsibility. Power is a large enough

topic and its implications so challenging that I have devoted all of chapter 3 to the subject. First, however, I will explore mutual vision and responsibility.

Mutuality modifies vision, describing how Marcus and I thought, felt, and responded to a shared vision for the congregation and for ourselves as pastoral leaders. Mutual vision gathers individual experiences, energy, understanding, giftedness, and creativity and offers them to God as gifts for the partnership and the community. This coming together allows us to discern and articulate a shared sense of call for our ministry. Marcus and I discovered that when vision is mutually owned, it grows and is clarified by the individual gifts we bring to it. Together, we share the benefits of those gifts as we pursue the vision for ourselves, our community, and our world. Often Marcus and I would ask each other to identify the energy we were experiencing; this question had to do with the amount of interest, excitement, and possibility each felt for the task ahead. This simple check offered us both some indication of the Spirit's activity among us. If we could identify an energy level that felt satisfactory to us both, that invited us to move ahead with some sense of positive outcome and worthwhile risk, then we would proceed. If not, we continued in discernment together. In some cases, we invited others to share this process with us. For example, the Pastoral Relations Committee might be invited to discern with us a new direction for our leadership. A worship planning team may be asked to come up with an idea for a worship theme or interpretation. Inviting others to share this process added to our clarity and understanding.

Mutuality can be visualized in simple mathematical terms. While two people working side by side might express their experience in the equation $A + B = AB$, with AB being the result of their collaboration, we experienced our partnership as $A + B = C$. My experience with Marcus was that working in mutuality transformed the product of our efforts into something completely new. Mutuality invited us not only to know ourselves at a deeper level but it also drew out of us untapped creativity and energy. By sharing the same vision, partners direct their efforts toward the same goal, maximizing potential and expanding the possibilities that the vision holds. In partnership, where or how an idea or vision starts becomes unimportant. Mutuality invites us to trust ourselves to each other, so that the end result—for good or ill—is something fully shared.

Mutual vision leads to mutual responsibility. When Marcus and I began our ministry together, many people assumed we would function much like other dual or multistaff clergy they had encountered. They expected that we would divide up the work between us, with each of us specializing in a variety of tasks. It came as a surprise to the congregation to hear us talk about mutually owned ministry, and we needed to interpret what that meant.

For our partnership, sharing the knowledge of and responsibility for all aspects of ministry was important for developing and maintaining mutuality. It signaled to the congregation that we were equally invested in the congregation's life and mission and that either one of us may be called on to respond with information, insight, and support. As a result, we did not divide up tasks into "mine" and "yours" but considered all to be "ours," with equal ownership in the joys and struggles that are inevitable. Likewise, the vision we articulated was one that we shared. Our mutual ownership of the vision strengthened and supported our sense of call to this ministry.

Mutually owned ministry within the congregation looks slightly different from that between pastoral partners. It is important that the congregation as a whole, like pastoral partners, has a feeling of ownership for the overall direction and purpose of the ministry we all share. However, unlike the work of pastoral partners who share pastoral care and are in some ways involved in all ministries, the ministry of members is carried out in different ways. Members, for example, can *choose* an area in which to serve and not feel obligated to work on the rest—a benefit of being a volunteer. Pastoral leaders, however, must be attentive to the workings of all congregational life, part of the responsibility of being a paid professional.

In many congregations, groups, committees, and boards compete with each other for the strongest leaders and the most resources. But in partnership, something different happens. In mutually owned ministry, while the congregation as a whole affirms and celebrates the entire ministry, the work of specific ministries can be done by small groups on the behalf of the whole. For example, Central Baptist Church currently has mission groups active in environmental justice; racism; affirmation and inclusion of, and advocacy for, gay, lesbian, bisexual, and transgendered people; partnering relationships in El Salvador; Habitat for Humanity; housing homeless families through Interfaith Hospitality Network; teaching English as a second language; and peacemaking. Not every congregation member desires or is able to participate in every mission group, nor is that necessary. Individuals who choose to commit themselves to these specific outreach activities do the work of these ministries. But because the congregation experiences mutuality in its relationships, the entire community has an investment and ownership in each one. Competition is replaced by cooperation, and the responsibility owned by a small group becomes shared by all.

Practically, mutually owned ministry for Marcus and me looked like this: both of us shared equally in the responsibility for worship planning and leadership; both of us attended congregational and Cabinet (elected officers) meetings, but we alternated, as much as possible, our participation in church board and committee meetings. For example, I would attend the Board of Communal Life meeting one month, and he would attend it the next month. Marcus would go the Board of Outreach meeting one month, and I would go the next. Occasionally, something else in our schedules would disrupt this pattern, but we worked intentionally to have both of us equally involved in the congregation's life. We wanted the congregation to experience the partnership, the impact of us both, whenever they saw or heard from one of us. As a result, we worked very intentionally to collaborate on all aspects of ministry; when one of us spoke, unless specified, the assumption was that we spoke for both.

While mutual vision enables leaders to set a direction, mutual responsibility speaks to how the leaders get there. Mutual responsibility encourages risk taking; leaders try more and varied things because they have the support of one another. Sharing ownership and responsibility opens up greater opportunity to experiment, to explore, and to envision new directions as leaders stimulate growth in each other. Working together—as pastors, and as pastors and congregation—prevents the isolation that so many clergy experience, one reason many pastors, particularly women, leave ministry. It also prevents insulation as pastors and congregation reach outside themselves to encourage each other and their community to grow. Because Marcus and I viewed ourselves as mutually responsible, we each had full ownership of any problem or situation; together we decided how to respond.

Mutual responsibility engenders vulnerable authority. It requires that we—congregation leaders and members—share both the opportunity and the risk of decision making. Pastors are granted authority by the congregation to lead, but in partnership that authority is exercised in a spirit of vulnerability. Vulnerable authority is open, permeable, transparent, and not rigid. It is an expression of trust in communal vision, wisdom, and experience of God's Spirit. Traditionally, the pastor may have been given the authority to set the direction for the congregation, for example. In partnership, those who serve as pastoral leaders recognize that their authority rests *in* the community. Leaders come to decisions knowing that they have only a part of the information, wisdom, and creativity necessary to lead, and so they invite congregation members to participate in meaningful ways. Mutuality and vulnerable authority take seriously the priesthood of all believers.

An example of vulnerable authority at work is revealed in communal discernment. As part of a congregational discernment process, congregational leaders asked Marcus and me to create an exercise to help them discover congregational priorities. We printed fake money (with our pictures on it) and gave it to congregation members. Then we asked people, with reflection and prayer, to put their "money" where their heart was. This exercise revealed people's passion and emerging priorities. Together we—leaders and congregants—uncovered the new direction we felt called to. In a similar process more recently, we gave the congregation hearts and asked them to express their understanding of God's invitation to our congregation for the future by choosing among several programmatic emphases. Where people placed their "hearts" told us all much about their passion for the ministry we were considering for the days and months ahead.

Vulnerable authority trusts that the energy and passion revealed in the congregation is in fact God's energy and passion. Therefore, we organize around this energy rather than our own agendas or the templates used by other congregations. Both pastoral partners *and* the wider partnership web that includes members understand there is no one right answer, no single solution. There are, in fact, multiple solutions to any given problem, and opportunities are created by even temporary solutions. The process may not appear neat and pretty, but it reflects the ownership of as many as possible for the good of all. Mutuality in relationship does not guarantee congregational support in decision making, but it does increase the chances of congregational affirmation as more people participate in the process and take ownership of the outcome.

Mutual vision and mutual responsibility are only possible with strong, intentional communication. At the beginning of our shared ministry, Marcus and I spent several hours each week in conversation. We talked about our visions, hopes, and fears, and how we understood who we were and what we were trying to do. We spoke openly and honestly about our own experiences, struggles, and joys, as well as our strategies for sharing our vision with the congregation. In that time, we came to know and trust one another and to live into the pastoral partnership we shared. We experienced a deep companionship in partnership, significantly different from the isolation often felt by solo clergy or even those in multiple-staff settings who do not experience mutuality. We reminded each other daily that we were not alone.

As we worked together over several years, we learned that communication continued to be essential. While we developed an internal shorthand that enabled us to more easily share the mechanics of planning meetings or making minor decisions, we continued to appreciate the value of frequent and direct communication for both our ministry and our personal lives. Because we were intentional about our communication with each other, we were confident that when one of us was present, the partnership was represented. Reviewing agendas together before a meeting, for example, allowed us both to offer thoughtful input that would be shared by whichever one of us would be present. If for some reason we had not had the opportunity to discuss a subject together before we were asked to respond to it, then we would simply say "I'm (or, "We're") sorry but we haven't talked about that yet. I'll be glad to get back to you as soon as the pastoral team can think about it together." Then, of course, we did just that. If an issue we had not talked about arose during a meeting where we were both present, many times we excused ourselves from the meeting to consult with each other before we responded. Rather than being annoyed that we delayed the meeting for a few minutes, congregants seemed impressed that we took mutuality and partnership so seriously. It also provided a good model for their relationships. Mutual vision and mutual responsibility required that we both remain engaged and committed to the entire work of the congregation. As a result, we offered the community our best effort to lead and serve together in every area.

Mutuality's Gift

Mutuality takes seriously who we are and what we have to offer. It lessens our individual burden of responsibility and frees us to discover one another and ourselves in a new and different light. We are not all gifted in the same way. In our partnership, Marcus often saw the big picture while I noticed the details. I often had the ability to conceptualize an idea, but Marcus was the one who actually figured out how to make it happen. When people work alone, the gifts they lack may be characterized as weaknesses. In partnership, however, people have the freedom to not do it all and the opportunity to work on strengthening gifts and skills within a relationship of loving support. Marcus encouraged my creative thinking even as I nurtured his attention to detail. We each still had strengths that were our unique contribution, while mutuality invited us to complement each other's gifts without threat or malice. Mutuality allowed us to try, grow, and even fail.

Whether any of us grows or fails, mutuality invites us to become full participants in the joys and responsibilities of partnership ministry. One responsibility Marcus and I felt was to resist the temptation to function independently, although we quickly discovered that we preferred working at and modeling collaboration in what we said and did. Although the careful communication necessary for mutuality demanded time and energy—a drawback for some people—we came to appreciate its benefits. Marcus and I found that the joys outweighed the responsibilities. Our experience revealed that the time we committed to effective communication and in building relationships where each one feels valued and respected was a worthwhile investment and became one joy of working together. Ultimately it reflected a deeper commitment to each other, to shared ministry, and to the congregation.

Turning the hierarchical model on its head as Jesus suggests in Luke's Gospel opens up possibilities for those who previously could not find their place within a system of domination. Mutuality takes seriously all who desire to be engaged in ministry, all who claim and offer their gifts, all who long to experience the communion of interwoven relationships that leads to wholeness and new life. Efficiency gives way to the important work of nurturing; expediency gives way to creativity. At the invitation to envision and respond, ideas and possibilities abound in unexpected ways. A group of people, creating a network of interwoven relationships where diversity is valued, own what originated with one individual. Mutuality calls out our strengths and makes room for our weaknesses, transforming both in light of Christ's example.

3 ∽

Power in Partnership

Redefining Relationships

∽Power is neutral, neither good nor bad. People reveal their values in the way they use power. In partnership, power is mutual. In partnership, power is unlimited; it increases when shared. In partnership, power is exercised in relationship; I notice that my power and how I use it is related to your power and how you use it. Partners do not use power to dominate one another; power is asymmetrical, not hierarchical. Power is collaborative, not competitive, and is exercised with mutual respect for and recognition of one another.

A Partnership Story

The issue of power seemed to arise almost immediately when Marcus Pomeroy and I began our pastoral partnership in January 1996. Within a few weeks we began to hear the question over and over again: "Where does the buck stop?" At first amused and later annoyed, we came to understand that inquiry as the ultimate question about power. Who is in charge? Who has responsibility? Who receives the credit, but we suspected more important, who gets blamed?

Marcus and I had begun to articulate a vision of mutuality—that is, equal ownership of the ministry we shared. But that seemed unnerving and unsettling to some congregation members. "How could power be used in a different way? What's wrong with the way we have always used power?" was the subtext. Who is really running the show, calling the shots? People in the congregation were so familiar with hierarchy and domination that imagining anything else seemed inconceivable and frightening.

Where does the buck stop? How can the use of power possibly be redefined? Marcus and I answered the questions immediately, repeatedly, dramatically, and, ultimately, convincingly for most people. We continued to describe our vision for sharing power. We began acting it out in congregational life. And we fashioned a sign that looked like a stop sign that read, "Buck Stop." On a Sunday morning, we placed it on the communion table located in the very center of the worship space. "This is where the buck stops," we gently told the congregation. "This is where the power resides: in our relationship with Christ, our community/communion, and with each and every one of you." This moment, and our effort to embody mutuality, was the beginning of redefining power in relationship, between both Marcus and me as partners in a pastoral team and between the congregation and us.

The question over where the buck stopped reflects the reality in which we all find ourselves. We live in a society where hierarchies are assumed and where domination is expected. We live in systems that have long embraced the idea that power is finite and therefore must be protected and preserved for the use of just a few. Our experience as dominator or dominated tells us that this is simply the way the world is; we are inexplicitly caught in a kind of "human food chain" where people prey on one another to gain position and control. Someone has to rule; everyone else must be ruled. Hierarchy ensures that those with power are limited in number; patriarchy ensures that they are male.

Partnership, however, imagines an alternative way of relating to each other and the created world. It imagines power shared and power multiplied; it imagines relationships that are free from domination and energized by mutuality. It imagines a truer reflection of God's realm in our lives as individuals and together as the church.

A Radical Shift

Jesus told the crowds and the disciples, "The religious scholars and the Pharisees have succeeded Moses as teachers; therefore, perform every observance they tell you to. But don't follow their example; even they don't do what they say. They tie up heavy loads and lay them on others' shoulders, while they themselves will not lift a finger to help alleviate the burden.

"All their works are performed to be seen. They widen their phylacteries and wear huge tassels. They are fond of places of honor at banquets and the front seats of synagogues. They love respectful greetings in public and being called 'Rabbi.'

"But as for you, avoid the title 'Rabbi.' For you have only one Teacher, and you are all sisters and brothers. And don't call anyone on earth your 'Mother' or 'Father.' You have only one Parent—our loving God in heaven. Avoid being called leaders. You have only one leader—the Messiah.

"The greatest among you will be the one who serves the rest. Those who exalt themselves will be humbled, but those who humble themselves will be exalted."

Matthew 23:1–12

Jesus said, "This is my commandment: love one another as I have loved you. There is no greater love than to lay down one's life for one's friends. And you are my friends, if you do what I command you. I no longer speak of you as subordinates, because a subordinate doesn't know a superior's business. Instead I call you friends, because I have made known to you everything I have learned from Abba God. It was not you who chose me; it was I who chose you to go forth and bear fruit. Your fruit must endure, so that whatever you ask of Abba God in my name God will give you. This command I give you: love one another."

John 15:12–17

No clearer demonstration of what God's realm is intended to look like exists than the one found in the life and ministry of Jesus. In a society that was both hierarchical and patriarchal, Jesus offers, through his actions and words, a liberating vision of power and its use. Jesus becomes the reference point for the transformation of assumptions about power; he redefines power in light of God's reign and invites us to do the same.

Jesus's description of the Pharisees in the opening verses of Matthew 23 is unflattering, to say the least. They are described as people who weigh down others with heavy burdens and who flaunt their spirituality to gain status. At worst, they are described as hypocrites who teach one thing and live another; at best, they strive to oppress people through the law. Either way, they use power to dominate others and as a way to demand respect within the community.

Jesus enjoins his community of followers to behave in a radically different way. He insists that they view themselves not as teachers but as learners, that they make no claim to power or authority. Rejecting titles for himself and for others, Jesus forbids the use of "father" (and even "mother") for human teachers, refuting the patriarchal social structures that demanded privilege and priority be given to males. He suggests a vision in which God alone is the leading, guiding, loving parental figure, in opposition to the hierarchy of power that elevates some above the rest.

Traditionally Jesus's use of the title *Father* for God has been interpreted not only to imply intimacy but also to associate God with a specific gender—male. The next "logical" assumption from this perception of reality is that males are like God (or even *are* gods). For this reason, Marcus and I chose to use inclusive-language biblical translations. Even though the term *abba* does translate into a masculine form (*daddy*), the intimacy of the image suggests that Jesus has in mind something different from a relationship between a distant, authoritarian parent and a weak, submissive child. This new images suggests a subtle shift in power from the traditional dominator-dominated relationship to a relationship that is closer and more compassionate and caring than imagined before. Late 20th-century biblical scholarship suggests interpretations of the above texts that radically reenvision assumptions about and use of power. By using the intimate name *Daddy* for God, Jesus denounces the absolute power the patriarchal religious leaders had assumed and rightfully assigns to the Divine a title the leaders had given themselves. By redefining relationship and language used by people to claim and use power for themselves, Jesus suggests a radical shift in how people relate to one another and to God. All people are placed on even ground and God is brought nearer. Language that had been used to separate and divide is reinterpreted as intimate; this intimacy invites us into new relationships.

Jesus's speech in Matthew's Gospel continues as he proclaims a vision of God's reign: "The greatest among you will be the one who serves the rest" (Matt. 23:11). Jesus proclaims a radical reversal of the status quo. Those who were considered to be "at the top" must now willingly, as a sign of their new understanding about power, take their rightful place "at the bottom." Those who benefit most from the hierarchy must serve those who are exploited the most. Not only is the structure of power changed but the use of power is also transformed. Power is no longer coercive but inviting; it no longer manipulates but serves. This new understanding of relationship and power opens the way for partnership.

Jesus carries this new interpretation even further in the words recorded in John 15:12–17. No longer are Jesus's followers called "servants" or "slaves," but they are renamed "friends." Jesus replaces relationships focused on power differences with relationships that celebrate each person as a gift, reshaping community in love that is selfless, empowering, and mutual. When the church takes seriously the invitation to friendship offered by Jesus, we find ourselves welcomed into a relationship built on shared power. In hierarchy, power is withheld from the servant, who is not entrusted with intimacy and close knowledge of the master. But in this new configuration, knowledge is shared and openness is encouraged. Relationships based on love, not domination, are hallmarks of God's realm.

Power Redefined in Partnership

While there are many ways to think about power, the experience of hierarchy and patriarchy has led many of us to believe that power is bad, that it can only be used to coerce and control (often described as "power over"). Partnership, however, discovers something new about power. Power in partnership might be described as "power with" and "power within," reflecting relational power and our ability to claim the power that belongs to each of us. Unlike hierarchical power that is restricted to a few and therefore assumed to be limited, power in partnership—mutually respectful, nonhierarchical relationship—is in fact limitless. Rejecting the myth that power is finite, partners discover that by sharing power it multiplies and grows, deepens and expands. Openness to give and to receive power leads to the creation of an ever-increasing number of opportunities through which power is shared and relationships are nurtured. Power in mutual relationships then—particularly relationships modeled

on the love of God in Christ—is power shared and multiplied
for the benefit of all. It is power that invites others into a growing network, or web, of relationships that generates creativity,
good will, and ultimately grace.

Such a radical departure from the domination model of
power naturally raises fears. One fear, of course, is of losing
power. When power is viewed as limited, fear of losing it is
legitimate. A second fear is change. If power is to be viewed as
limitless and mutual, then the system, whether society or the
church, that supports such a model will have to be vastly different from the current one.

Power in partnership is mutual; it is communal, not individual. While each of us possesses personal power, we offer it
to each other and to the work we do together; amazingly, this
increases both our sense of our own power and that which we
share with others. It is collaborative, not coercive or competitive. What Marcus and I discovered in sharing power was not
that we replicated the same ideas or insights or visions but that
what emerged out of our collaboration was something entirely
new. When my idea and my partner-colleague's idea become *our*
ideas, each of us was tapping into energy and creativity neither
had alone. What emerged was something that neither of us had
previously conceived but discovered only in our willingness to
share power with each other. Such power multiplies, making
it readily available to both use and to give away; the more we
experienced this, the more confident we became that sharing
power with others simply increases it, widening and deepening
its ability to transform.

In partnership, partners must claim their legitimate power
and share it. While power in partnership is always mutual, it
may not be identical. While people may have equal power, that
power may not be expressed or used in identical ways. At times
asymmetrical power is an appropriate response to a situation
or person. (Asymmetrical power acknowledges that leaders
may have roles, functions, even access to information different

from other leaders or congregants.) Leaders do not use power or role to set themselves above or against other leaders or the congregation; rather, they consider these resources for working with the congregation to deepen its spiritual and communal life. There were times in our pastoral partnership that Marcus and I agreed that I would be the one to lead and speak on our behalf, because it was important that my voice as a woman be heard in the face of gender-based assumptions. At other times, because he felt strongly about a particular action or about a response to a situation, I agreed to support him, even though the resulting direction may not have been my first choice, had I been acting alone. Occasionally illness or personal crisis necessitated expressions of asymmetrical power. In those moments, temporarily stepping in for the other actually becomes an act of love and grace. At times one partner, out of expertise or passion, may take the lead; one may defer so that the other may grow. Most important is that the use of power be mutually agreed upon, that all parties in the relationship remain honored and respected, that they know what they are doing and why, and that they communicate openly and make decisions together about how to act. This keeps the use of power fluid and flexible rather than predictable and rigid. Without intentionality and clear boundaries, asymmetrical power can easily revert to power over; should the balance tip too far, predispositions for hierarchy most likely will take over. Leaders committed to partnership remain vigilant. While power may shift, what remains constant is the commitment to mutuality in relationship; partner-leaders remain insistent that power be used to strengthen and add to, not take away from or diminish relationships. By attending to relationships, leaders remain intentional about how power is being used in the partnership and why. Partner-leaders trust each other and communicate carefully. It reflects their redefinition of power in light of Christ's example and in relationship to one another and the world.

Power used by a partner-leader within a congregation may also be expressed as asymmetrical. Here again, power is shared and not used to dominate, even though the power expressed by the pastor as leader may look different from that expressed by a congregation member. Power shared between leaders and congregants moves throughout the weblike structure of the partnership relationship. Where and when it emerges is dependent on call, passion, energy, and the movement of God's Spirit.

An example of this shared power and leadership comes from community organizing, as described by Marcus Pomeroy:

> When effective community organizations confront hierarchical power, e.g. the mayor's office, the hierarchical power will often try to isolate "the leader" and then co-opt that person through favors or special influence. The community organization resists this effort by sharing leadership and power among the organization's members. The hierarchical power never knows where the leadership will emerge and as a result is forced to negotiate with the organization as a whole. It is the *organization* that has power, not the individuals within it.[1]

Movement of power and leadership within the congregational web results in power that is mutual and asymmetrical; it is power shared and power multiplied.

What Power in One Partnership Looked Like

Because people in our society have been conditioned to expect power to be used and experienced in hierarchical, dominating ways, we are often uncertain about the practical form mutually shared power might take. In workshops and learning opportunities on partnership and power, Marcus and I have frequently used what we call the Kiss Game to demonstrate the reordering of power. The group is paired off, and pairs are invited to grasp each other's hands (right hand to right hand or left to left), placing elbows on a table or flat surface between them. Many identify this as a typical arm-wrestling stance, although that language is carefully avoided. The pairs are then told that whenever the back of their partner's hand touches the table, they will receive a candy kiss. The object is to try to get as many kisses as they can. They are given a time limit and told to begin.

What inevitably occurs is a traditional arm-wrestling match. Because the pairs are not matched according to strength or size, in most cases one person dominates the game, amassing the most candy while the other person has few, if any, kisses. What is interesting is the assumption that the object is to acquire as much candy as possible for the individual, not for the team. No one has told them this; rather, it reflects what they have been socialized to do.

Some who interpret this as a competition and deliberately choose not to be competitive simply sit the whole thing out, preferring to have no candy at all. Roughly one pair in every group will discover that if they simply take turns placing the backs of their hands on the table, they will each receive the same number of candies and will, with very little or no effort, gather the greatest rewards every time!

The Kiss Game illustrates the need to think creatively about reordering and sharing power. Over and over again, people act out of their conditioning within the domination system, without recognizing it. Hierarchy is like the air they breathe. The use of power to dominate is so pervasive and so assumed that people usually do not even notice it is happening; most of us think it is necessary. We feel challenged when we begin to notice domination. The struggle comes when we try to dismantle the system that is in place in an attempt to live into a web of relationships that we have yet to discover. We do not usually know what it will look like, which requires us to be open to new possibilities and new ways of being in relationship.

Jesus's invitation to shared power suggests a transformative model for looking at and being in the world. His vision for the last to become first, for the least to become greatest, for outcasts to sit at the table with him redefines what power looks like in relationships. In the same manner, the church is called to live in stark contrast to the domination systems inside and outside the church. Partnership is an attempt to live out now what was modeled in Jesus's ministry—what is possible when people resist the dominant systems of power and oppression and live into the vision and hope of God.

In partnership, when power is redefined as mutually shared, ministry looks different than it did before. In Marcus's and my shared ministry, we found that questions of mutual power were raised most often in relation to money, time, information, and language.

Knowledge is power. Who knows what about money and who decides how and when it is used reflects the power systems at work in any institution, even the church. For Marcus and me, the issue of money was raised in conversations about the church budget and about our salaries. Early on in our partnership, we noticed that concerns about the budget or financial matters were most often addressed to him and not to me. In paying closer attention to patterns and habits, we discovered that men dealing in money matters consistently approached Marcus for his input and opinion and assumed I had neither interest nor experience that would benefit them; they were simply living out the social construct that women do not need to know about money. (The congregation did not happen to have women in financial leadership positions at that time.) Because Marcus and I could share power, we actively resisted the sexism implicit in such conditioned behavior; we intentionally redirected conversations and our own participation in decision making to emphasize the mutual nature of our ministry.

Salaries were an additional money matter that needed to be addressed. Domination assumes that salaries are based on seniority, which is defined by education, age, experience, longevity, and gender. While we were full partners in this ministry, Marcus worked more hours each week than I did. He was also older and had more years experience and more education. I, however, had greater longevity in the particular congregation we served. Knowing that money can seriously corrupt and cripple a relationship, we insisted that the differences between us be viewed as shared commodities, not as a basis for differentiation. As a result, our salaries were the same with adjustments made for the number of expected work hours. While this particular scenario is unique to us, it points to an important reality for all partnerships that involve remuneration. According to the values of hierarchy, greater significance is attributed the one who makes more money. Partners must be careful to resist this assumption and to work out suitable financial arrangements that are fair but at the same time reflect the alternative values they are attempting to model. Our interpretation of these values and the agreements that reflect them were important for congregational understanding and support.

As we mutually shared power, Marcus and I could address the concern about time and confront the question of whether speed equals value. A hierarchy values full-time employment over part time and believes that faster is better, that quantity is more valuable than quality. Partnership, however, considers the team; mutual power increases efficiency, input, creativity, and energy because where one of us was, the team's cumulative influence was present. Although sharing information within the partnership was time consuming, it increased the power available to each of us individually and to both as a team. It allowed for shared access, shared ownership, shared response, and shared decision-making in the congregation's life.

As pastoral partners, Marcus and I believed that sharing information was a reflection of shared power. Knowing the same things about groups and individuals in the church so that we might offer everyone our most thoughtful and gifted response was important. Mutual ministry invited the congregation to

approach either one of us for pastoral care or for information, because we were both involved in the congregation's life
and ministry. Certainly, differences between Marcus and me
prompted congregants to come to one rather than the other. We
would remind people that their concern or joy would be shared
with the other pastor, however. That way they knew they were
supported by both and could approach either at any time with
the confidence that we would understand something of their
situation. Because we shared information about church boards
and mission groups, the congregation experienced the cumulative effects of our partnership even if only one of us was present. Again, Marcus and I spoke for the partnership only when
we were confident about our joint response. Such information
sharing demonstrated sharing power. It communicated that
we worked together. Likewise, sharing information demonstrated that we resisted patterns that would divide us, and it
reduced unhealthy behavior (triangulation, for example) in the
community.

Language—spoken, written, even body language—conveys
much about how an individual and a group views power. Partnership demands that language be inclusive, that what is said
and how it is said reflect the desire to be in mutually respectful
relationships. While gender-inclusive language was not new to
Central Baptist, the language Marcus and I used to describe the
pastoral team was new. When a colleague would say, "Let me
introduce you to *the* pastor," either Marcus or I would gently
correct the speaker by responding with something like, "I am *one*
of the pastors at Central Baptist Church." We described ourselves
as "pastoral partners" (as opposed to marriage partners; we are
both married, but not to each other) or part of the "pastoral
team" (which included the student interns we often mentored).
We resisted being referred to as "copastors," believing that the
term carries its own assumptions—often two individuals working on parallel tracks—which is different from the mutually
owned ministry of partnership.

Yet changing language is never enough to change ingrained behavior. Marcus and I learned that where we sat in a group conveyed something about our understanding of power. For example, for a meeting taking place around a table, we would usually sit in the middle rather than "at the head," and we noticed that the dynamic could change when we sat apart from each other in a room rather than side by side. We even physically changed places during a conversation to redirect the eye contact of an individual or a group, so that our message was consistent: in partnership power is shared, and we actively resist and work to undo the hierarchy in our midst.

Prophetic Transformation

It is my belief and experience that reordering power in partnership is both the most difficult and the most prophetic transformation that this model offers to individuals and to the church. Identifying and dismantling the domination system present in the church and in our society disrupts the systems of power in a transgressive way. Rather than only resist the domination system, however, the church must take the lead in this dramatic action if indeed the church is to remain faithful to the call and witness of the transformative leaders of its past, particularly to Jesus. This reordering makes partnership prophetic.

Throughout the centuries prophets have dared to speak directly to the powers that dominate society, whether political, economic, religious, social, or all of these. In the name of God and on behalf of the community, the prophet offers the cry of resistance, points out oppression, struggles to dismantle conventional systems and envisions a transformative relationship to power. From Moses to Jesus, prophetic visionaries capture a glimpse of the divine hope for all creation and proclaim that hope in radical ways, raising the consciousness as well as the consternation of those who hear them. Prophets resist the systems of power that oppress, and they offer life-giving vision to those who long for hope.

Partnership is a prophetic model that actively works to dismantle the domination of hierarchy and patriarchy and to embody mutually shared power that opens us to new spiritual life. Partnership requires a dramatic shift in how leaders and congregants think and speak and act; it is an active resistance to the powers that dominate the church and our lives.

The prophet's task is not simply to point out what is wrong but to offer something in its place. Partnership offers a fresh way of relating, both individually and communally, that realigns power, stimulates creativity, and opens people to one another and to God. In resisting the current systems of power and speaking a word that liberates us from the powers that prevail, partnership is prophetic. Partnership's liberation is found in the invitation to share power, but also in its insistence that society and structures be viewed from a vantage point different from the cultural norm.

Partnership's vision for shared power is drawn directly from Jesus's own sharing of power among his followers—women and men, poor and wealthy, ill and well. Jesus's example, while set in a particular context, not only transcends that context but transcends all contexts, offering a vision and a model of life-giving relationship for all people; a model for a new humanity, a new wholeness, a new embodiment of God's reign in the church and in the world.

4 ⌒

New Spiritual Community

⌒The result of dismantling oppressive systems and imagining alternatives, establishing relationships based on mutuality, and examining and redefining the nature and use of power in community is to create space—spiritually, structurally, relationally—for the birth and growth of new spiritual community. Through this process, which results in a new paradigm, leaders who choose the partnership model find a deeper expression and fuller understanding of God's Spirit, healthier relationships, and a new embodiment of God's presence in our midst. As we endeavor to envision what is yet to be, we open ourselves to God's invitation to see one another and ourselves in fresh ways; we allow ourselves to be moved and guided by God's Spirit in ways that both surprise us and give us life.

A Partnership Story

So what does new spiritual community look like? What would that mean for us at Central Baptist Church? These questions had been asked by people in the congregation more than once, as Marcus and I encouraged them to think of partnership reaching beyond the two of us, envisioning a web of mutuality linking the people of Central Baptist to one another and to those outside the congregation's walls with whom we discovered connection through shared concerns, such as racism. But the congregation wanted a blueprint, a "how to" manual they hoped we would provide to help them move toward new community. The only problem was *none* of us knew what this new community looked like or how to get there.

Marcus and I began to spin out our vision of new spiritual community sitting in circle at a meeting of Central Baptist's leaders. I unraveled an arm's length of the yarn I was holding and said: "I'm connected to Marcus because we share a pastoral partnership." Holding onto the end, I tossed the skein of brightly variegated yarn to him. "I'm connected to Jim," Marcus said as, holding onto his own section, he tossed the yarn across the circle to Jim. "We sing barbershop together in church." It was Jim's turn: "I'm connected to Norm because we work on the church finances together." The skein was passed again. Smiling, Norm responded: "And I'm connected to Cindy because she's my daughter."

And so it went. Back and forth across the room, people around the circle identified ways they were connected with one another. Some were known to those present—hobbies shared, relatives, work or group connections. And others were surprises. Who knew that those two went to the same school, that these two had family history in common? Person after person, relationship after relationship, the yarn spun out its rainbow web, a symbol of the multiple layers of our connections and relationships with one another in the faith community.

After the web became quite complex, Marcus and I began to ask the group questions: "What do you notice about the web?" "It's beautiful," came the reply. "What is necessary for it to form and to stay in place?" we asked. "We need to notice who's connected to whom, and stay connected," someone else remarked. "What happens when someone drops their piece?"

we wondered and asked a particular person to do so. What all of us noticed was, while the web sagged a bit, it did not fall apart. In fact, the other strands held it up. "How about that side giving it a tug?" we suggested, pointing to a portion of the group. The web began to tighten and to shift. Everyone was affected; the shift eased the tension for some, made holding on more difficult for others. Still holding our yarn, we began to explore what the web suggested about nonhierarchy, mutuality, power, and new spiritual community. We experienced ourselves thinking and speaking, visualizing and understanding partnership in a dramatic and exciting way.

Partnership values mutuality and a new way of being in relationship (nonhierarchy), opening us to the transforming work of God's Spirit. Partnership is birthed from within the community, not imposed upon it. Together we discern God's invitation to a new way of being in relationship with one another. We allow ourselves to be woven by the Spirit into this holy web.

New spiritual community is the result of partnership; by dismantling hierarchy and redefining power, we create space for newness and the transforming action of God's Spirit. As partnership grows, creativity expands, people and structures change, relationships deepen, and vision flourishes. God invites us to community in an interconnected web of relationships that begins with the Spirit moving in our midst.

Weaving the Partnership Web

There was a centurion named Cornelius in the Italian cohort stationed in Caesarea. The household of Cornelius was full of God-fearing people; they prayed to God constantly and gave many charitable gifts to needy Jewish people.

One day at about three in the afternoon Cornelius had a vision. He distinctly saw an angel of God enter the house and call out, "Cornelius!"

Cornelius stared at the angel, completely terrified, and replied, "I'm at your service."

The angel said, "Your prayers and offerings to the poor are pleasing to God. Send a deputation to Joppa and ask for a person named Simon who is called Peter. He is staying with a tanner also named Simon, whose house is by the sea."

After the angel had departed, Cornelius called together three members of the household, explained everything to them and sent them off to Joppa.

About noon the next day, shortly before they were to arrive in Joppa, Peter went up to the roof terrace to pray. He was hungry and asked for something to eat. While the meal was being prepared he fell into a trance. Peter saw heaven standing open, and something like a large sheet being lowered to earth by its four corners. It contained all kinds of animals, birds and reptiles.

A voice said, "Stand up, Peter. Make your sacrifice, and eat."

But Peter said, "I can't, my God. I have never eaten anything profane or unclean."

The voice spoke a second time and said, "Don't call anything profane that God has made clean."

This happened three times, then the sheet disappeared into the heavens.

Peter was still pondering the vision when Cornelius' deputation arrived. They had asked directions to Simon's house and were now standing at the door. They called out to ask if Simon, known as Peter, was there. While Peter reflected on the vision, the Spirit said, "A deputation is here to see you. Hurry down, and don't hesitate to go with them. I sent them here."

He went down and said to the deputation, "I'm the one you are looking for. What do you want?"

They answered, "Cornelius, a centurion—an upright and God-fearing person, respected by the Jewish people—was

directed by a holy angel to send for you. We are to bring you
to the household of Cornelius to hear what you have to say."
Peter invited them in and gave them hospitality.

Peter left the next day, accompanied by some of the co-
workers from Joppa. They reached Caesarea the day after.
Cornelius was waiting for them, along with his household
and many close friends.

As Peter entered the house, Cornelius met him, dropped
to his knees and bowed low. As he helped Cornelius to his
feet, Peter said, "Get up! I'm a human being, just like you!"

While talking with Cornelius, Peter went in and found
many people gathered there. He said to them, "You know it's
unlawful for a Jew to associate with Gentiles or visit them. But
God made clear to me not to call anyone unclean or impure.
That's why I made no objection when I was summoned. Why
have you sent for me?"

Cornelius answered, "Four days ago, I was here praying
at this hour—three in the afternoon. Suddenly a figure in
shinning robes stood before me and said, 'Cornelius, your
prayers have been heard and your charity has been accepted
as a sacrifice before God. Send to Joppa and invite Simon,
known as Peter, who is staying in the house of Simeon
the tanner, who lives by the sea.' So I sent for you immediately and you were kind enough to come. Now we are all
gathered here before you to hear the message God has given
you for us."

So Peter said to them, "I begin to see how true it is that
God shows no partiality—rather, that any person of any
nationality who fears God and does what is right is acceptable to God. This is the message God has sent to the people
of Israel, the Good News of peace proclaimed through Jesus
Christ, who is the Savior of all.

"You yourselves know what took place throughout Judea,
beginning in Galilee with the baptism John proclaimed. You
know how God anointed Jesus of Nazareth with the Holy

Spirit and with power, and how Jesus went about doing good works and healing all who were in the grip of the Devil, because God was with him. We are eyewitnesses to all that Jesus did in the countryside and in Jerusalem. Finally, Jesus was killed and hung on a tree, only to be raised by God on the third day. God allowed him to be seen, not by everyone, but only by the witnesses who had been chosen beforehand by God—that is, by us, who ate and drank with Christ after the resurrection from the dead. And Christ commissioned us to preach to the people and to bear witness that this is the one set apart by God as judge of the living and the dead. To Christ Jesus all the prophets testify, that everyone who believes has forgiveness of sins through this Name."

Peter had not finished speaking these words when the Holy Spirit descended upon all who were listening to the message. The Jewish believers who had accompanied Peter were surprised that the gift of the Holy Spirit had been poured out on the Gentiles also, whom they could hear speaking in tongues and glorifying God.

Then Peter asked, "What can stop these people who have received the Holy Spirit, even as we have, from being baptized with water?" So he gave orders that they be baptized in the name of Jesus Christ. After this was done, they asked him to stay on with them for a few days.

The apostles and the community in Judea heard that Gentiles, too, had accepted the word of God. As a result, when Peter went up to Jerusalem, some of the Jewish believers took issue with him. "So you have been visiting the Gentiles and eating with them, have you?" they said.

Peter then explained that whole affair to them step by step from the beginning: "One day when I was in the town of Joppa, I fell into a trance while at prayer and had a vision of something like a big sheet being let down from heaven by its four corners. This sheet came quite close to me. I watched it intently and saw in it all sorts of animals and wild beasts—

everything possible that could walk, crawl or fly. Then I heard a voice that said to me, 'Now Peter, make your sacrifice and eat.' I replied, 'I can't, my God. Nothing profane or unclean has ever entered my mouth!' And a second time the voice spoke from heaven, 'Don't call profane what God has made clean.' This happened three times, then the sheet and what was in it was drawn up to heaven again.

"Just at that moment, three couriers stopped outside the house where we were staying; they had been sent from Caesarea to fetch me, and the Spirit told me to have no hesitation about returning with them. These six believers came with me as well, and we entered Cornelius' house. He told us he had seen an angel standing in the house who had said, 'Send messengers to Joppa and bring back Simon, known as Peter; he has a message for you that will save you and your entire household.'

"I had hardly begun to speak when the Holy Spirit came down on them in the same way she came on us in the beginning, and I remembered what Christ had said: 'John baptized with water, but you will be baptized with the Holy Spirit.' I realized then that God was giving them the same gift that had been given to us when we came to believe in our Savior Jesus Christ. And who am I to stand in God's way?"

This account satisfied them, and they gave glory to God, saying "God has granted the repentance that leads to life—even to the Gentiles!"

Acts 10:1–11:18

At first glance, this extended text appears long and cumbersome, rounding back on itself and telling the same story again and again. The temptation is to skip through it, to fast-forward to the finish. Often that is indeed how this passage is read; the repetition of the story pushes us to reach the end.

It is the repetition, however, that spins out an example of the partnership web in congregational life, a very model of new spiritual community. This is a story of radical change, first in one individual's life, then in another, and finally in the larger community. A web of interconnection slowly begins to develop; space opens up for new ideas and new relationships. Change in one leads to change in another. At first, there appears to be no natural connection between Paul and Cornelius. But as their encounters with God's Spirit are revealed, their lives become first connected and then intertwined. Each person's experience adds meaning to the other's. Cornelius does not know why he is instructed to send for and listen to Peter. Peter cannot comprehend the mysterious vision or the invitation to visit Cornelius. They start by each telling their stories. They look to one other for understanding and truth. They discover their hearts are opened to new ideas, new understandings, new experiences of God's Spirit. Both are transformed! And it is their transformation that invites a change in others, first in a small group as the story is told again, and then in many, many more listeners. Spiritual community is formed as Peter, Cornelius, and their communities open themselves to a new understanding of God discovered *only* in their connection with each other.

New spiritual community comes to life when pastors and congregants view each other as integral, share stories, and value each other as gift and revelation. We are invited by God's Spirit to embody a faith that lives and grows in relationship—in relationship to God, ourselves, and others. Neither Peter nor Cornelius could make sense of God's wisdom without the help of the other, and the greater community did not understand what was happening until they saw their friends' transformation for themselves. We are drawn into communion with one another, so that we might offer each other a clearer picture of God and a deeper understanding of the Spirit's movement.

Peter and Cornelius discover that, to fully comprehend the deeper meaning of the Spirit, they not only need each other but they also must open themselves to possibilities they had not considered and people with whom they had not interacted before. Peter cannot imagine eating the foods placed before him. ("We've never done it that way before.") Cornelius had no idea who this Peter was. ("They aren't like us.") Yet by trusting God's Spirit, they find themselves drawn together in an intricate web that opens them to new ideas and understandings of themselves and one another. But this web did not stop with them. The experience of transformation extends to those around them: "God has granted the repentance that leads to life—even to Gentiles!" (Acts 11:18). Mutuality, diversity, and interrelatedness open us to new spiritual community, to embodying a fuller expression of God's reign in our midst.

Partnership Creates Space for Newness

In becoming partners with one another, in choosing to build relationships that are intentionally nonhierarchical and mutual, we open ourselves to discover the web's gifts. As our connections deepen, we find space within ourselves and between ourselves and others that we may have never experienced before. Creativity expands as we embrace a new paradigm and as we offer our gifts to one another. Structures change as we work to remove the systems that keep us separated from each other, and we can begin to envision new possibilities for relationship. Our interaction with each other takes on greater significance as we begin to appreciate the depth of our interrelatedness. Personal and communal vision born out of this new experience of self and other begins to grow. The movement of God's Spirit is not only noticed within and among us but it is also anticipated and expected. The connections we discover in the web invite us into relationships with each other. Responding to the flow of life and energy that emerges from these relationships, the web expands to include even more people. Partnership creates space—both interior and exterior, for individuals and for the community—for something new.

While this experience of new energy and creativity had been expressed in the pastoral partnership Marcus and I shared (see chapter 2, "The Gift of Interdependence") seeing it blossom within the Central Baptist Church community as well was exciting. The congregation was invited to participate in a planning event that began on a Friday evening and concluded late on Saturday afternoon. Members and friends were asked to share memories and significant experiences from the past, both from personal history and from their experiences within the church. Together we charted an enormous timeline that spanned decades, and women, men, and children wrote dates and memories that were significant to them and to their faith. Births, deaths, graduations, and weddings began to fill the long sheets of paper that covered the walls of the church social hall. National and global events—wars, elections, governmental policies, marches, and protests—also were added. Baptisms, memorial services, child dedications, significant events in the congregation's life—such as agreeing to mortgage the property to send money to inner cities after Martin Luther King Jr.'s, assassination, becoming a Sanctuary Church for undocumented refugees during the war in El Salvador, declaring Central Baptist Church a Welcoming and Affirming Congregation, joining the Alliance of Baptists—all found their places on the wall. We stood back and looked at our timeline together. It charted our lives and witnessed to our faith. It reminded us of the times we hung together and those times when we fell apart. The timeline recorded our strengths and weakness, our sorrows and our joys. But most of all it reminded us that we were community, interwoven in life and faith, and that, like other times in the past, together we could once again be something new.

That was how the weekend began, with remembering who we were both as individuals and as a community together. Over the hours we shared, we continued to dream, wonder, and create together. We discovered that our congregation had no lack of imagination. Someone suggested we buy the local middle school and transform it into low-income housing. Someone else dreamed of a community arts center housed in our space. Still another envisioned solar panels on the roof to provide our own source of environmentally friendly energy. Someone else longed to encourage new spiritual growth by creating house churches. We talked about selling our building. We thought about changing the makeup of our staff. The creativity and the energy generated by envisioning together opened up minds and hearts like never before. Inviting people to speak, listen, dream, and discern together gave birth to the beginning of new spiritual community. The web was being woven. It was starting to happen in our midst.

The synergy was amazing. Right then and there, several small groups formed to wonder aloud about what they had heard being spoken in and around them. These groups reported back and were combined as we discovered more than one group being led in a similar direction. Next, this new configuration of groups met, sharing ideas, dreams, and leadership and seeking together to understand the creative energy that was present in a dynamic and powerful way. It was invigorating. It was exhausting. It was fun!

Partnership gives birth to new spiritual community by of ferlng a model of opening ourselves to each other in trust. That openness and trust invite us to be creative and responsive to the Spirit's movement in and between us. As creativity expands, structures that have long served the status quo must be reevaluated. Asking whether new vision can actually come to life within the systems and power arrangements already in place is an important question for the community. New ideas can transform old structures. It is possible that a new vision must be supported in an entirely new way. At our planning event, as small groups continued to envision and report back to the whole group, it became clear that the old structure could not easily nurture some of these new directions and ideas. Rather than assign these new eruptions of energy to existing boards that had not envisioned them to begin with, it became evident that these small groups ought to continue to meet, if only to flesh out their vision. As a result, new structures came to life to support new vision, and leaders within the existing structure worked to build relationships that encouraged the emerging life and energy.

In one group, members said they were invested in "nurturing spirituality" within our Central Baptist community. Drawing together a unique combination of people who had not made connections before, this group envisioned the transformation of a storage space into a meditation room. With enthusiasm, they gave voice to a vision for this space. Eagerly they committed to make this dream reality. One person volunteered to clean the room, disposing of various documents and furniture. Others offered to paint the room and buy new furniture. Yet another offered to communicate this vision with the congregation and to create a sign-up sheet so individuals and groups could reserve the room. Someone else channeled the details about what was taking place through the appropriate congregational structure, so that both leaders and congregants were informed and decision-making responsibilities honored. Within a few months, a lovely, inviting, reflective room to pray, rest, and meditate was created. The congregation was encouraged to donate additional art, music, and literature to make the space their own. New spiritual community was emerging among us in ways that were tangible and transformative. The web of relationships was widening and deepening as individuals were drawn to one another by God's Spirit at work in community.

Relationships deepen as people discover new ways to connect to each other. In the example above, the catalyst for connecting was a shared desire for nurturing spirituality. The mutuality of partnership invites us to trust ourselves to each other, to treat one another and to experience ourselves as valuable gifts. When we dare to remove structures that support domination and difference, we find space where we can recognize the richness of gifts and diversity at home in each human being and in the creation of which we are a part.

Deepening relationships no doubt involves an element of risk because partners make themselves vulnerable. In honesty, one can discover and be discovered; however, willingness to become open and vulnerable is key: on either an individual or a communal level, we enter into partnership because we are seeking a new way of being in relationship in the world. We choose to be vulnerable, then, as a means to a greater end. We allow ourselves to be open to each other in hope that everyone might be changed.

What emerges as creativity expands, structures change, and relationships are deepened is a clearer vision and purpose for us and for our community. Just as neither Cornelius nor Peter could fully understand God's invitation without the other, neither can we fully comprehend God's call to us as community without the benefit of relationships that bring us together. Our willingness to grow and our commitment to the growth process leads us to clarity of vision. Articulating an idea or a desire in community provides the opportunity for others to respond, further clarifying the vision and allowing others to express affirmation and support.

At Central Baptist Church individuals typically express a call to outreach ministry within the experience of the worshiping community. When someone experiences a pull in a new direction, they usually share this invitation with the congregation, often during worship at the sharing time called "Celebrations and Concerns." As people hear this call expressed, they too begin to think about whether or not they sense an urgency or interest in this concern. When as few as two or three discover a similar passion for this ministry, they meet to discern more fully the invitation of God's Spirit they sense they are receiving. If it becomes clear this direction inspires energy and life, others are welcomed to join. If the group discerns that sufficient excitement around this particular area is not present, then it is set aside, at least temporarily, with the possibility that it might be raised again. Central Baptist's ministry to homeless people, for example, arose when one person articulated a concern and others who shared this passion joined the effort. New spiritual community is given birth as the church actively discerns God's call and invitation to us and when we seek direction together, viewing ourselves as part of an interconnected web. We find insight and wisdom as it rises within the faith community and beyond as well as within us.

What New Spiritual Community in One Partnership Looked Like

The church's response to God's call is expressed in new spiritual community—the multidimensional web, the fluid weaving of individual and communal lives that enables God's Spirit to move freely among and through people, both drawing us close and flinging us out to create new connections and new webs. What new spiritual community in partnership looks like is a reflection of those who participate in it. For Marcus and me, it took the shape of a pastoral team, two individuals united by call, vision, and purpose sharing one ministry.

A few years into our partnership, Marcus and I were asked by the youth to host the talent night they were providing for the congregation. Wanting to share the playfulness of the evening and to demonstrate further what it meant to live into this partnering relationship, we decided to capitalize on another point of mutuality: our love for M&M's. Together Marcus and I designed and gathered the necessary props for our costume. The night of the talent show we appeared wearing two tee shirts sewn together to look like one large shirt, with the classic M&M's logo on the front, and one very large pair of pants made out of M&M's-designed fabric. With an arm discretely placed around each other's shoulder, we looked, in fact, like a large-bodied, two-armed, two-legged, two-headed M&M. The event was very fun, and our costume said something people understood: we were two distinct persons joined in a relationship that brought creativity, passion, and life together in a brand new way. As members of the Central Baptist community began to recognize just how different *leadership* looked in partnership, they also began to see how different they could—in fact, did—look as they grew into new spiritual community. While people did not dress up as one *bag* of M&M's, they began to name their connections as "partnerships" with one another and with groups outside the congregation.

Communion describes the interconnectedness we experience in partnership, as individuals and for our community as a whole. Marcus and I began to refer to Central Baptist as a "communion" of faith, taking seriously the sacramental nature of our relationships woven in the presence of Christ. Marcus and I believed that the web of relationships formed between and among us contained sacred elements—truth and trust, risk and grace, love, vision, and hope.

The web brings ideas, concerns, and people together that previously had seemed unconnected. It weaves threads that hold us to one another in ways that may surprise us. For example, the congregation's decades-long history of relationships in El Salvador taught us that proximity is not necessary for us to be connected. A recent visit from our Salvadoran friends reminded us of this as, after sharing their struggle and their vision and knowing our own struggle to live in this new vision, they said, "When we feel overwhelmed and discouraged, we think of you. And we know that you walk beside us, that you share our hope, and that we are never alone." That is new spiritual community: discovering mutual relationships, sharing vision and purpose, exchanging spiritual and emotional energy, experiencing the presence of God's transforming Spirit in our midst.

The web—asymmetrical, dynamic, multilayered, reaching both inward and outward—is the transformative image for new spiritual community. The image became the focal point of a worship series about partnership at Central Baptist Church. (See appendix B, "Web Visions: Leadership as Community; A Sermon Series.") On one wall of our sanctuary, called the Worship Commons, we strung rope back and forth, up and down, over and under other stands to create a compelling vision of the web of relationships. Lighting from the top and sides projected the web's shadows on the wall behind, adding depth to the sense of interconnectedness. Against this striking backdrop, we worshiped, prayed, sang, and spoke about the web of relationships growing in our midst, about leadership as community, and about the work of God's transforming Spirit among us. This visual reminded us that in the web those traditionally assigned to the edges because of difference or distance discover that they are, in fact, linked with those closer to the middle. Without a definite center, the web shifts and changes; as energy and life flows along its interconnecting threads, the web is tugged—it challenges us, connects us, and binds us to each other.

The web also changes us. It moves us from the individualism and isolation of hierarchy to the mutuality and relatedness of community. The web enables us to see and make connections that were not previously evident. The web of relationships grew at Central Baptist Church a few years ago when we invited our Salvadoran friends to visit with us in the States and introduced them to a group of young adults, called The Simple Way, who lived and worked among Philadelphia's poor. The Salvadorans discovered a solidarity of suffering, and as the relationships grew and deepened Simple Way members in return visited El Salvador. At the same time, we at Central Baptist began to understand that our relationship with the poor in Central America was directly tied to our relationship with the poor in our own city. The dynamic web expanded; our experience of new spiritual community deepened. The web became the image of God's activity in community, a communion of spirits in Christ.

A Joyous Birth

New spiritual community is the hope and the goal of partnership, the life-giving outcome of the effort to dismantle hierarchy and to replace its stagnant, narrow, rigid structures with the rich, wide fabric of mutuality. The community's weblike shape and design change with amoeba-like fluidity, encircling those previously left on the margins and inviting in all who desire to have a part. As partners discover new life between themselves, envisioning it for others as well is only natural.

Just as Cornelius and Peter in the Acts of the Apostles needed to be open to the movement of God's Spirit, new spiritual community requires openness to God's Spirit and willingness to be receptive to God's invitation to us. This Spirit undoubtedly pushes us toward new expressions of God's reign. New spiritual community most certainly looks, sounds, and feels very different from anything we have experienced before. New spiritual community requires discernment to clarify the Spirit's invitation. As new ideas and vision arise within our community, members ask, "Is this life giving? Does this point us toward the way of Christ? Does this make sense in the context of God's movement among us in the past?" When the answer is yes, then the community proceeds with confidence, careful to recognize that we must continue to ask these questions of each other and of ourselves individually along the way. And if the answer is no, then we must reevaluate and discern what God's invitation truly is, so that the vision of new spiritual community might remain clear.

One indication that new spiritual community is among us is the experience of strength and vitality as a community. God's Spirit opens our hearts and fills our imaginations with dreams, visions, and possibilities never before conceived. It stretches us and remakes us; it does not leave us unaffected. Cletus Wessels writes of this transformation of the Spirit: "If the wind that is dismantling the structure of the church is truly the breath of God, then instead of destruction there will be a new Pentecost, a new heaven and a new earth. This new beginning calls for a new paradigm."[1]

The web emerged at Central Baptist as the confines of structures were breeched and individuals and groups reached across false barriers to share ministry and to offer their gifts. Instead of saying, "This is our task, and we'll just have to figure out how to do it," more boards ask, "Who has the gifts for this ministry? How can we get them involved, even though they are not members of this committee?" That expansiveness was evidenced throughout the congregation as well. More frequently, we began to hear the congregation saying, "That's not your [the pastors' or a particular board's] problem; it's ours [the congregation's], and we'll just have to wrestle with that together." This reflects mutuality in ministry that grows as people see themselves connected in a multitude of ways. Likewise, web relationships began to deepen our connections outside the congregation as we asked, "What other groups share this value and are working toward this vision, and how can we share the work with them to make all of us more effective?" Like Peter and Cornelius, we experienced a deeper interrelatedness emerging that drew us into each other's story, vision, and ministry, leading us in new directions by God's Spirit.

This is the experience of birthing new spiritual community: openness to the space created by partnership, discovering anew or for the first time the transforming nature of the Spirit of God. We embraced nonhierarchy, mutuality, and a new understanding of power, not only because those things are significant in and of themselves, which they are. But we embraced them because we had hoped for, and discovered that, partnership's purpose is to give birth to new spiritual life. Nonhierarchy is not an end in itself; neither is mutuality, although both are good. Partnership inevitably led to something greater than itself: new spiritual community—the web. Partnership in ministry is a transformative vision. It leads us into a deeper connection with each other, wherein we come to a fuller understanding of ourselves, each other, and God.

5 ⬡

Living into
the Vision

⬡My purpose in writing this book is to invite both pastors and congregations into a new way of thinking about ministry, leadership, and the future of the church. I want to offer both clergy and laypeople a fresh model that is life giving, empowering, and transformative. That model is partnership.

Partnership as a model for ministry originated out of a longing and vision for nonhierarchical leadership. When my colleague Marcus Pomeroy and I began our ministry, few resources were available to guide our thoughts and actions. So we began by writing our own definition, making our own map. As the vision we shared with Central Baptist Church unfolded between and among us, pastors and congregation alike, we began to experience transformation—as individuals and as a community of faith. To our delight, partnership worked! And as others outside Central Baptist noticed its life-giving effects, we began to receive inquiries about what we were doing. Other leaders and congregations beginning similar journeys asked for advice and support, widening the partnership web. My hope is that this book will serve as a beginning place for those who hear God's invitation to lead in fresh, creative ways and who long to live into a vision that will bring a new spirit to the church.

A Partnership Story

Marcus Pomeroy and I met in a hotel suite because the restaurant was filled with a noisy crowd. It was late in the evening after a busy day. The Pastoral Search Committee of Central Baptist Church had flown Marcus Pomeroy to Wayne, Pennsylvania, to talk with him, show him around, and discern whether he was the one they should invite the congregation to consider as a new member of the pastoral team.

They already had one pastor—me. They were looking for another. The committee wanted Marcus and me to introduce ourselves to each other; to check each other out; to speak, listen, and discern. Our meeting felt like what I imagined anticipating an arranged marriage might feel like. Is it going to work? Can we get along? Will it be all right?

Both Marcus and I came to that meeting that night with experience and vision, hope and hurt. Although we had very different experiences of pastoral ministry, we shared some of the same disappointments and frustrations with the local church. We had been solo pastors of congregations and knew the loneliness that often accompanies that experience. We had been in multiple-staff situations where hierarchy stifled our creativity and swallowed our energy. We had felt both blessed and betrayed. We took turns telling our stories openly and honestly; we were both very aware of how much was at stake.

"I won't be anyone's 'associate,'" I declared. "I want to be seen and treated like an equal; I'm not going to work *for* you." "I want a relationship of mutuality," he replied. "I want to be able to trust you and to have you trust me." "I like to preach," I went on. "So I want to have the very same access to the pulpit as you. No more, no less. I want preaching to be shared." "I agree with you," Marcus answered. "I like to preach, too. If we are to be seen as equals, we should share that responsibility equally."

And so the conversation continued, each of us articulating hopes, fears, and something of our pain—all things that led us to this point, to this conversation, to this vision for ministry at Central Baptist Church. The process continued to move forward, and Marcus was called to join the pastoral partnership at Central Baptist. In 1996 we began to live into a new way of leadership, a journey we shared for 10 years. We did not know then what partnership looked like; we were not even sure what it was. One of the very first things we did was to articulate a definition, so that we had vision and language guide us as we began. We had hope and a sense that this model for ministry was a gift of God's Spirit, an invitation to coax into being a tiny portion of the unfolding reign of God.

Our experience of partnership taught us many things. Most important, Marcus and I learned that partnership cannot happen unless it is freely chosen. It cannot be prescribed but must grow out of a genuine desire for mutuality, a new way of being in relationship. We learned that partnership requires intentional, difficult work. Dismantling and resisting systems and structures that have been in place for centuries is a daunting task, demanding vigilance and steadfastness. And we learned that partnership is life giving. We did not, and most likely could not, know where this path would lead us, but it brought us to unforeseen relationships, vision, and energy. We believe that this model of ministry reflects the model found in Jesus Christ. Our experience also taught us that it is God's Spirit within and among us that invites us to this new life.

Accompanied by the Spirit

"Now I am going to the One who sent me—yet not one of you has asked, 'Where are you going?' You're sad of heart because I tell you this. Still, I must tell you the truth: it is much better for you that I go. If I fail to go, the Paraclete will never come to you, whereas if I go, I will send her to you. When she comes, she will prove the world wrong about sin, about justice and about judgment. About sin—in that they refuse to believe in me; about justice—because I go to Abba God and you will see me no more; about judgment—for the ruler of this world has been condemned. I have much more to tell you, but you can't bear to hear it now. When the Spirit of truth comes, she will guide you into all truth. She won't speak on her own initiative; rather, she'll speak only what she hears, and she'll announce to you things that are yet to come. In doing this, the Spirit will give glory to me, for she will take what is mine and reveal it to you. Everything that Abba God has belongs to me. This is why I said that the Spirit will take what is mine and reveal it to you. Within a short time you won't see me, but soon after that you'll see me again."

John 16:5–16

These words of Jesus, meant to comfort the confused and distressed disciples, no doubt did little to ease their anxiety and concern. Their world was changing; Jesus was leaving them. They did not understand why and were uncertain about what would happen next. They were used to Jesus's physical, visible companionship and guidance. Now they needed a new way to think about and be in relationship to each other and to the Christ. The Spirit would come as an inner companion, Jesus promised, and it would be available to transform their hearts and lives.

We too live in times of confusion and uncertainty. Jesus's promise of the coming Spirit prepares us for change and guarantees that we will be accompanied. This very same Spirit calls us to understand the world, God, and ourselves in new, exciting ways. Partnership is a response to this Spirit, whose invitation to us is to model relationships that are transformative for us and for the life and ministry of the church. By choosing partnership we receive, and in turn offer, a life-altering gift.

What We Learned in One Partnership

In addition to learning that partnership must be freely chosen, which I discuss below, Marcus and I learned that mutual relationships are only possible with intentional, hard work. Dismantling hierarchy and resisting patriarchy are difficult tasks. The labor demanded our attention and our strength. Marcus and I noticed that we had more energy for it at some times than at others; we spoke of having a "thin margin" when the struggle seemed great. But discovering we were accompanied—by one another, by congregants, by God's Spirit—in the midst of difficulty was comforting; partnership ensures that none of us labors alone. At times our own internalized oppression surfaced and got in the way. For example, I was tempted to defer to Marcus when I felt challenged. At other times he considered rescuing me if he perceived that I, as a woman, was being verbally threatened or attacked. Occasionally we tripped over our own egos, momentarily forgetting that what ultimately nourishes us is the depth of our relationships in the communion of the living Christ.

Marcus and I learned that living in mutuality when the world around us lives in hierarchy was difficult. Taking seriously the invitation of partnership to reorder power and relationships within the church context means we not only struggled to change our own relationships but we found ourselves nurturing change in the church as well. This was difficult work, which is why, I suspect, this change comes so slowly to any church. Honest self-reflection, building consensus, and respecting and honoring everyone in the web were difficult practices. We learned that only those who choose to embody a radically different model and to persevere when confronted with resistance actually make a difference. We learned that we must be intentional and faithful to the vision.

As Marcus and I struggled to birth a new vision, we learned that what we were experiencing was nothing less than new life. Quite simply, partnership was fun! We loved what we were doing and how we were doing it. The struggles and heartaches of our days in ministry, common to every pastoral leader, were sprinkled generously with laughter and playfulness, creativity and joy. Two carrying a load was easier than one. The congregation owning what was rightfully theirs in the web of relationships rather than leaving their struggles and hopes on the doorsteps of the pastoral staff was healthier. In mutuality the weight is shared, the burden minimized, and companionship is experienced along the way.

Marcus and I learned that with the joy of companionship comes the energy of creativity. Individuals are so much more when they work *together* than when they are on their own. Marcus and I found that when risk and reward was shared, courage and strength grew. Supported, we dared to reach out in new directions, take on significant challenges, hear biblical texts afresh and preach them with greater boldness and life. As leaders, our strengths and weaknesses served to complement and enhance one another; this realization fostered confidence and grace.

Marcus and I also learned that partnerships are not created overnight. A significant investment of time and energy must be made in the initial startup of a partnering relationship as pastoral partners, and pastors and congregation, get to know each other and share their vision and hopes for their relationship. Knowing each other's strengths and weaknesses and getting a feel for each person's rhythm and style take time. But this time is a valuable and necessary component of partnership; it helps ensure that the relationship is built on honesty.

Is Partnership for You?

Not every leader or congregation will *want* to choose partnership. Marcus and I have always been clear that this is *one* model, not *the* model. Each pastoral leader and congregation will have to ask themselves the question, is partnership the right leadership model for us? Partnership ministry begins, and possibly ends (if there is no support for it), with pastors. While congregations

seeking new pastoral leadership may indeed search for leaders who can embrace partnership, as was the case at Central
Baptist, congregations whose pastoral leaders are satisfied with
conventional hierarchal leadership will be frustrated in pursuing
congregational partnership without pastoral support. Individual
congregants *can* practice nonhierarchical mutuality in their
personal and professional relationships. Individuals *can* embrace
partnerships in small groups and friendship circles. But without
pastoral leadership, I find it difficult to imagine partnership
being practiced at any depth within the church. Still, visionary
congregants who are attracted to this model might want to invite
their pastoral and church leaders to reflect together on this book
as a way of introducing others to this model for leadership and
congregational life.

In addition to requiring pastoral affirmation and enthusiasm,
partnership is possible for visionary and risk-taking pastors who
love to work collaboratively. Pastoral leaders have to be able to
envision this model (or something like it) for themselves and
the congregation, be willing to try new things, and truly desire
to work alongside others. Partnership requires pastoral leaders
to have a healthy sense of self—a satisfied ego and positive self-
esteem. The pastor is not the sole leader and decision maker
in partnership, the pastor must be able to offer her or his gifts
for the whole, not for personal recognition or gain. Maintaining appropriate leadership boundaries is an important skill for
partnership. People—even well-meaning ones—will test and try
this model; as pastors resist traditional patterns of relationship
(such as hierarchy), they will need to act and to communicate
without ambiguity.

Pastoral leaders who choose partnership will need to be
creative. How partnership looks in your congregation and
ministry will be different from how it looked for Marcus and
me and Central Baptist Church. There is no one right way to
do this—that is part of the fun! You must be open to following
the Spirit's lead, committed to a path of spiritual growth. You

must also be deeply passionate about justice for yourself and for others, because partnership dismantles ingrained patterns of power and relationship. This dismantling is a difficult challenge but well worth the transformation possible if your heart is in it.

Just as partnership is not for all pastors, neither is it for all congregations. Congregations I know that are working on some form of partnership desire to move in new directions, have a strong congregational spirit, and welcome challenges. For many, this is not the first outrageous thing they have attempted. They are congregations that thrive on following the Spirit, doing new things, responding in creative ways to injustice. These groups, like their partner-leaders, are also visionary, risk taking, and have a healthy sense of their communal life. Partnership congregations are forward thinking, open to change, and passionate about justice for themselves and for the world.

Pastors and congregations considering partnership ministry will want to identify congregational leaders who will make strong partners. These leaders must desire to work out of a new model, must be willing to lead change, and have spiritual maturity. Congregational members who are creative, willing to make mistakes and try again, and enjoy working collaboratively will make excellent leaders for partnership.

Passion for Partnership

Partnership begins with the desire, passion, and commitment to envision leadership and ministry in an entirely new way. It also begins with prayerful consideration—seeking God's direction for yourself and for your congregation. You may be the pastoral leader. You may be a member of the congregation. You may have been involved with your church's ministry for years or are just new to your community of faith. You may have served this congregation for some time and feel the need for a new leadership style. Or you may be a part of a pastoral search committee looking for a new leader with a fresh vision for leadership and congregational life. You alone may hold this vision or you may be surrounded by others who share your desire for new life. No matter what your role in the congregation, partnership begins with passion and prayer.

As you consider partnership, begin by articulating your vision. Say it out loud. Write it down. Struggle over the wording so that you can be as precise as possible about the invitation you are experiencing. Marcus and I prayerfully worked on our definition over a period of weeks, carefully ensuring that our language communicated as much as it possibly could about what we were discerning in those beginning days. We then shared the definition with several leadership groups, which gave us the opportunity to say it aloud, to respond to their probing, to refine our language yet again. Each time we gained clarity about what partnership might look like, until we felt that we had captured the spirit of our call.

As you write your vision, be concise. Say as much as you can in as few words as possible. Pay attention to what you *are* saying, and notice what you are *not* saying. Who does this definition include—pastors, leaders, the congregation? What is the goal or purpose for this change? What will partnership do to and for you as leaders and as a congregation? Consider language and meaning. Partnership redefines the use of power and invites congregations to web relationships. Make sure you can articulate this. You will want to use this vision—only a sentence or two—as a vehicle for telling others what you are all about. Make the vision something you can use for years to come. Finally, spend time with what you have written. Pray with your vision statement. By "pray with," I mean use your vision statement as the focal point of repeated contemplation. Is this what God is truly inviting you to be, to do? Ask God for a sense of peace, blessing, and excitement about the work ahead of you. Be confident that your work is infused with God's Spirit.

Freely Choosing Partnership

Our definition of partnership begins with the words *freely chosen,* words that came to have great significance in our model for pastoral leaders and the web of congregational life. While these words come at the beginning of the definition and are a prerequisite for partnering relationships, I leave discussion of them until this point in the book because their importance is experienced throughout all facets of partnership.

Partnership must be chosen, most certainly by the individuals who lead and ideally by the community they serve. Partnership cannot be coerced but must be the reflection of a genuine, God-directed desire to dismantle the structures that have long dominated the church and to seek alternatives in mutuality. Partnership must be sought after, envisioned, longed for by the heart. The work required to achieve mutuality in the culture of most churches is too difficult to pursue halfheartedly or without deep commitment. New creation does not just happen. Nurturing transformation into being requires hope against the odds and passion in the face of opposition. The opportunity to choose freely is essential and where commitment to partnership begins.

Marcus and I freely chose partnership ministry. At the beginning, we did not completely know what partnership looked like, where it would take us, what impact it might have on each of us and on congregational life. But we had hope and vision for a new way for men and women to be in relationship and a desire to dismantle an oppressive, destructive system that had hurt and limited us both. In addition we shared a passion for teasing out just a bit of what we understood to be God's reign in our midst. Choosing partnership is important; we learned that we must never assume partnership, but that we must intentionally choose it over and over again so that our relationships might thrive.

We chose partnership each day as we decided whether to act unilaterally or collaboratively. Choosing partnership once does not automatically make us experts at living it. When I had information that Marcus did not have, for example, I had to choose whether or not to share it with him. My decision reflected whether I was choosing partnership or something else. The mutuality inherent in partnership directed me to share the information, knowing information shared is power shared, even though conventional patterns of hierarchy would warn that power shared is power lost. Over and over again, in situations as simple as this, we chose to be in partnership with one another.

And what about our congregation? Some people had a sense that they freely chose partnership when they hired Marcus to be a part of the pastoral team. The Pastoral Search Committee, on behalf of the congregation, sought someone who could join me in embodying this vision, even though at that point none of us was sure what partnership would look like. For those who caught the vision early on, their affirmation of Marcus and me as pastoral leaders was a choice for partnership.

Other people in the congregation needed more time and a clearer sense of the vision. While they supported the *idea* of partnership, they felt as if they did not initially have a choice, because they did not fully understand what they were being asked to choose. Opportunities for education and experiencing partnership in pastoral leadership and congregational life helped these people understand the vision. Appreciating the value and experience of partnership in our communal life took some people a long time.

Since partnership became the model for leadership at Central Baptist, newcomers have been added to the congregation. These people were not a part of the original conversation about moving in this direction. Explanations about partnership became a part of our visitor and new-member welcoming so that they too could understand who we were—as a pastoral team and as a community—and make a choice about entering into this type of relationship.

And some ultimately chose not to engage this vision at all. They remained participants of Central Baptist, with varying levels of activity, but resisted the partnership that was unfolding among us. As a result, Marcus and I and, at times, the rest of the congregation experienced them as out of sync with congregational values and ways of relating even as we felt out of sync with them. The congregation was still able to work and grow together, but more effort was required to maintain partnership values in those relationships.

The first time Marcus and I taught an adult-education class about partnership, we began with "freely chosen," knowing even then, early in our ministry together, that *choosing* was an integral step toward partnership. But it is important for choices to be made with as much knowledge as possible. Subsequently, we saved the discussion about "freely chosen" until the end of our series of classes about partnership. We learned that ongoing conversations about partnership lead to informed choices that have integrity and meaning. Nonetheless, the decision to choose partnership for everyone in the web, in reality, is not made once but all along the way. People choose this model by the way they live, by the way they relate to one another, by the way they respond to the invitation to new life.

Commitment to Partnership

Once you—pastoral leaders and congregations—have chosen partnership, enlisting the support and commitment of others is important. Create a small group of eager, honest, creative, visionary advocates. You want and need others to catch this vision. A small group of advocates would

- share your excitement and hope for change,
- give you honest feedback and offer encouragement,
- run interference for you as you take risks in leadership,
- act as advocates for change.

The support of others who can talk with you about this new way of leading and becoming community will be of benefit to you. In partnership you are no longer the lone voice. As others join your vision for new life, you can model collaboration.

Create a network of personal support for yourself as you lead your congregation in this new direction. Ask your partner/spouse (if you have one), a close friend, or a clergy colleague to accompany you in this journey. Their support and encouragement will be invaluable to you. They can pray with and for you and for your congregation. They can laugh and celebrate with you, as well as hear your frustrations and challenges. Partnership is not about going it alone. Good companionship will make the traveling much more enriching.

As you invite others to make a commitment to partnership with you, remember that communication is essential. To get your vision of partnership off to a successful start, communicate clearly and often with everyone. People want and need to know what you are doing and thinking, and why. So tell them! Use every medium available to you to share your vision for nonhierarchical, mutual ministry. Preach a sermon series or two or three (see appendix B for examples), write newsletter articles, teach adult education classes, and post your vision statement along with an explanation on your church Web site. Talk about partnership in each board and committee meeting you attend. Visit small groups throughout the congregation—seniors, women's, men's, youth groups, and tell them all about this exciting and challenging way of relating that you are envisioning for your community of faith. People will ask questions; they will get excited. Be honest. Tell them what you hope for and how you plan to begin. Invite them to conversations—formal and informal—as a way of gaining support and welcoming them into the process. Marcus and I learned that it is critical for as many people as possible to know what is happening and to be invited to participate in Jesus's transforming ministry.

And as you are talking about partnership, start living it. Begin to put into practice the vision you have created. Try something—anything! Marcus and I began by teaching an adult education class with our partnership definition as the focal point. Week by week we pulled apart the phrases and talked about their potential meaning for our life together. The class gave the Central Baptist community a chance to have deeper conversation with Marcus and me, to talk with each other, to dig into what we were doing and why at the start, and to help interpret for themselves this new direction God was calling us to. We created two separate curriculums to talk about partnership, and we used them a few years apart. (See appendix A: "Partnership: Vocabulary and Vision for Congregational Life; An Adult Learning Curriculum.") The initial curriculum introduced the concepts at the heart of partnerships—nonhierarchy, mutuality, power, and new spiritual community. Later on, we developed a learning process that was more reflective. It drew out people's experience with partnership and explored the web relationships that had emerged in our midst. This gave people a chance to get on board at different points and to grow in their understanding. By the time we taught the second set of classes, most people had been watching our partnership unfold for a couple of years, so they too, in addition to Marcus and me, had firsthand experience to share about the how partnership affected them and the community.

As you begin to live into your commitment to partnership and to try new things, you will make mistakes. We did. At times we thought we had communicated well with the congregation and had not. There were days Marcus and I thought we understood each other and we did not. At one point the two of us had been saying so much about partnership that someone asked, "Could we stop *talking* about this and *do* it?" Mistakes should be expected as any of us take the risk of becoming transformative leaders. If nothing else, when mistakes happen you can be sure that you have people's attention! What you think is a mistake may in fact turn out to be an exciting discovery.

For example, over a two- or three-year period, Marcus and I worked with congregational leaders to formulate a new direction for our life together. Marcus and I had a notion of our congregational priorities, but we could not seem to get any further in the process. What seemed like an endless "plan to plan" was making us weary—until at one point Marcus and I stopped planning and started to notice what was actually happening in Central Baptist's life. We began to notice where energy and movement were present in the web. This was a shift from directly leading where *we* wanted to go and instead discerning where God was already leading us. What we had thought was a failure in our process turned out to be an expansion of the mutuality of web relationships. Our role was not to decide where to take this congregation but to invite the community to follow God.

As you live into partnership, be prayerful and attentive to God's Spirit. Marcus and I learned that we could only see a portion of the vision at a time. Trust that God will lead you and those around you to new insights and new challenges; you will learn much along the way. Stick to your plan *even as you change it.* Partnership is an organic expression; it unfolds and emerges as you live it. The image of the web came to Marcus and me only after we began to experience our interconnectedness. As you notice the changes that are happening around you, be attentive to the changes you experience within yourself. Ask yourself:

- How does it feel to be intimately connected to others?
- How comfortable are you as a nonhierarchical leader?
- Where do you find yourself getting stuck in old patterns?
- What feels liberating and invigorating?

Expect God to be present in what you say and do. One thing Marcus and I discovered was that partnership was just plain fun! The congregation recognized the joy we shared in serving together; our joy became a gift for the entire community.

As our congregation was transformed by partnership, a deeper sense of connectedness emerged. For many in our congregation, Central Baptist Church is family in the richest, most profound sense of the word. New relationships began to form as individuals saw themselves connected to each other in new ways, weaving a web of relationships that shifted yet embraced all. Structures were challenged and stretched as partnership bumped up against them. Small, short-term task groups emerged and later dissolved as needs arose and were met and as the congregation moved beyond those concerns to tackle something new. Communication between existing structures increased, with ever-increasing interaction that reflected the growing web. Creative thinking flourished in the space created by partnership. All ideas were valid; all possibilities considered. Dreams were encouraged and visions shared, whether it was the call of many or the call of one. In partnership the congregation sought to hear God's voice in the midst of the community; diversity gave us a clear picture of the One who was among us.

Roadblocks and Pitfalls to Partnership

As you live into your partnership vision, you will inevitably experience roadblocks or pitfalls along the way. Some of these are consequences of age-old congregational processes, like traditions and bylaws. Some will be created, either intentionally or unintentionally, by people. And some struggles, believe it or not, you will create for yourself.

As described in the "buck stop" story in chapter 3, an inevitable roadblock can be the misuse or misunderstanding of power in partnership. Power in partnership is mutual; it expands as people share it. Power in partnership is relational and limitless, modeled on the love of God in Jesus. Nonhierarchy and mutuality are difficult things for people to grasp. Confusion will likely occur over how power in partnership is appropriately expressed and what nonhierarchy in relationship looks like. It is not difficult to understand that as a result of nonhierarchy, individuals and structures change; it is just hard for people to understand how.

Leaders, both clergy and laity, can help people understand nonhierarchical power by modeling its use themselves in relationship to one another and to the congregation as a whole. The more times people saw Marcus and I use our power collaboratively and the more we pointed out that we were doing so, the easier it was for them to grasp and appreciate.

Poor communication is another pitfall to partnership. People need to know what is happening and why. Failure to communicate leads people to feel left out, uninformed, and unappreciated. It can lead to misconceptions about partnership—particularly about power and how it should appropriately be used in partnering relationships (because knowledge is power, people who are feeling out of the loop end up feeling powerless). Articulating your vision and your hopes for congregational ministry is important. It is also important for members of the faith community to be invited to be part of the journey.

Partnership is supported and nurtured by God's Spirit thereby deepening our spiritual lives. Without giving attention to the need for embracing and integrating the gift of God's Spirit into our lives, the inevitable lack of spiritual support for a leader will become a roadblock. People called to partnership need to experience a call to change and must truly believe that transformation is possible. This call and belief must be supported by prayer, Bible study, reflection, meditation, and the encouragement of the community, all of which lead us toward new life. Transformation of individuals, communities, and structures is a spiritual exercise; to thrive on the journey of change, partnership leaders must discover avenues for spiritual support.

Another roadblock to partnership can be the ego needs and insecurities of the leaders. Partnership demands that the leader work in collaboration with other leaders and the congregation. Leaders who expect to be at the center of congregational life will struggle with this model. They may feel disappointment, a sense of being disrespected, and uncertainty about their role and authority. Instead of moving in new directions, leaders with unmet ego needs may repeat old patterns in an attempt to feel comfortable and in control when things get difficult. Partnership's rewards are found in community, not in individual effort or recognition. The person who needs to be singled out for recognition and reassurance of his or her importance will likely be unsatisfied when the community's celebration is focused on what is shared and how it has emerged. The partnership leader rejoices in the energy and vitality of the web—a representation of community—and while she or he appreciates affirmation, the leader is not defined by it.

While there are undoubtedly others, the last roadblock I will mention is the lack of congregational support. It is unlikely that you will receive unanimous support for the life-changing notion of partnership. Change, giving up old patterns and ways of relating, also introduces in congregations fear of the unknown, loss, the need to let go of the past, and uncertainly about newness. These feelings are all very real and significant, and they need to be dealt with openly and repeatedly. Your best pastoral care skills will be helpful as you allow people to talk about what this new way of relating means for them, what they lose, and what they hope to gain. The more you allow these feelings to come out and be expressed in the open, the clearer the places of resistance will be and the more easily that resistance can be addressed. It is important for partner-leaders to be aware of the level of resistance partnership is generating. Ask: Who is having the most difficulty with these changes? Why are they struggling? How many resisters are there? What do they need to see, know, or do in order to lower their threshold of discomfort? Answers to these questions will help leaders respond to the congregation's needs and will also make partner-leaders aware of what they are up against. Marcus's and my experience in most cases was that resistance faded as people experienced the effects of partnership for themselves and the community. When we experienced resistance that seemed immune to our efforts to transform it, we ultimately settled for knowing what the problem was and whom it was coming from.

What Transformation in Partnership Looks Like

One of the marks of transformation is congregational discomfort; if people are uncomfortable chances are you are doing something right! Choosing partnership will instigate a season of transition for both leaders and congregation; dis-ease is to be expected and, in many cases, a sign of growth.

As you experience change, also look for evidence of new life. You can expect to hear and use new language as you and those around you begin to talk about partnership, mutuality, and web relationships. To hear congregational leaders talking with each other about creating nonhierarchical board structures and making the connections between our congregation and other groups in our surrounding community was invigorating for Marcus and me. New ideas, questions, and energy emerge as people catch on and become excited about the possibilities for partnership in their community.

One area where Marcus and I experienced the need for change was in congregational structure. Web thinking pushed the boundaries of our board and committee structure and forced the congregation to look at new and creative ways to be connected. Partnership invites a reordering of congregational life, and, because this realization emerged over time, congregational leaders and pastors took time to think and talk about restructuring. The congregation eventually agreed to suspend a portion of the congregational bylaws that specifically defined boards and groups, so that it could free itself from the past and move into the future. For example, the bylaw requirement that each board have a chairperson and vice chairperson was relaxed to allow for boards that wanted to experiment with shared leadership. The congregation began to use more short-term, appointed committees to do specific tasks, such as envisioning a new music ministry and seeking new leadership. Making the framework more flexible allowed the congregation to experiment without losing the benefit of the familiar structure and to make mistakes without creating chaos.

As Marcus and I moved deeper and deeper into partner leadership, we discovered that communication became easier, more natural, and more integrated into our personal and congregational routines. While at first saying and hearing all we needed to from one another seemed to take much time and effort, a rhythm eventually developed that made communication both more efficient and more essential. We knew, for example, that we needed to touch base before each board meeting, so we developed a kind of shorthand that allowed us to do that more efficiently. Our shorthand ranged from coming to our conversation with lists of concerns already made to simply knowing each other well enough to be able to anticipate issues and responses. We also realized the dangers of not communicating well. We were unprepared for specific questions in meetings a few times, for example, which reinforced our need to be as prepared as possible. As Marcus and I experienced the benefits of mutual support and shared leadership, we became even more eager to deepen the connections that formed between us all. This increased ease in communication also allowed all of us to gain greater clarity about our vision and our vision statement. Talking about it and living into it sharpened our vision and deepened our understanding, making the vision clearer and more compelling to those around us. Because of better communication, members of the congregation who felt like they were on the edges of the community began to "get it." They became excited about partnership and the new spiritual community arising within us. All of this—ease of communication, deepening vision, clarity of purpose—strengthened and expanded the web so that partnership moved beyond clergy and congregational leaders to the faith community as a whole.

As partnership catches hold and the relational web draws in more of the congregation, the new life that is emerging in the church begins to be noticed by people outside the congregation. Central Baptist congregants took partnership into the community, sharing the model with other groups and organizations and inviting others to try it in their personal relationships. In these ways, the web continued to expand, connecting people and groups beyond our congregation. As others came to know the work we were doing at Central Baptist, other congregations, clergy, and pastoral search committees began to contact Marcus and me for advice, insight, and direction for their own transformation. Life encourages life, and we were always happy to offer whatever wisdom and encouragement we could to others along the way.

Partnership: An Invitation to Transformation

In many ways, neither Marcus nor I knew what we were getting into when we met for the first time to talk about partnership in that hotel room many years ago. And yet, in a way, I suspect we did have some idea. What I envisioned was an alternate way of doing ministry, of being connected to those around me in deeper, more authentic ways. What I longed for was to more truly express my call and use my gifts, to embody a call that embraced my gender as well as my spirituality. What I hoped for was in some small way to make a contribution as a woman in ministry to both women and men in ministry who—experiencing isolation, loneliness, and spiritual incompatibility with the structures of hierarchy and domination—might be seeking another way to embody God's reign in and through their lives. For me, partnership has been a response to these desires as I have experienced them in my own life. In the living out of this partnership, transformation of my life and ministry and of one congregation has been possible.

Partnership invites people to look critically and lovingly at themselves and the church and to envision transformation. Looking critically at themselves within the partnership model, people dare to recognize culture's imprint on their lives and relationships and seek to identify how hierarchy and patriarchy have taken up residence. Looking critically at the church, people expose the many ways in which the church has co-opted the systems of hierarchy and patriarchy as its own. Partnership deconstructs oppressive powers and structures, freeing faith communities to reclaim a christological foundation for something new. Jesus offers a model different from the one the church has come to reflect—a model of love and acceptance that seeks to recognize the gifts each person offers the world.

Partnership draws out the redemptive goodness inherent in human nature, inviting people to become gifts to one another. Not willing to dismiss the church, but desiring new life, vision, and hope, people of faith seek in partnership a new expression of God's Spirit in order to offer a clearer reflection of God's reign. As a model for ministry and congregational life, partnership invites people to a deeper understanding of their own calls, relationships, and way of revealing the incarnation in daily life. Partnership invites people to transformation and leads them to new spiritual community in the grace and hope of Christ.

Partnership embodies nonhierarchical mutuality in the church and a vision for pastoral leaders and for the larger community of faith. Central Baptist Church continues to work at it and to live into it, because in partnership the congregation has found freedom, life, and movement of God's Spirit unlike that in any other ministry it has experienced. I believe others in the wider church long for a new way of leading and that congregations are open to building community in deeper, more meaningful ways. As leaders and congregants, our *talk* about

doing something different is meaningless if we cannot begin
to discover ways of *being* something different—embodying the
values and vision we see in Jesus's life and ministry. The church
needs to be a leader in bringing God's reign to life. Transforming individuals and systems *is* possible when we are responsive
to God's Spirit. Partnership calls us to such a transformation as,
attentive to the Spirit's movement, we embody new life.

Appendix A

Partnership:

Vocabulary and Vision for Congregational Life

An Adult Learning Curriculum

∽ "Partnership: Vocabulary and Vision for Congregational Life" is a curriculum for an adult educational opportunity. Eight sessions highlight the core ideas and values that make up the particular vision and understanding of partnership as both a leadership style and a model for congregational life that Marcus Pomeroy and I developed with Central Baptist Church, Wayne, Pennsylvania. Each session assumes a 55-minute time frame but can be adapted to fit individual congregational needs.

While this curriculum centers on the particular definition of partnership explored in this book, feel free to adapt the ideas here to your own specific definition of partnership as it emerges out of your vision and congregational life. In addition to using them in a weekly adult education class, pieces of this curriculum can be used in other venues. Choose just the texts for a Bible study or a worship preparation group. Use some of the group exercises (such as creating the web or lowering the dowel in session 8) as discussion starters at a youth group, board, or congregational meeting.

Partnership requires creativity. It is my hope that you will use this resource in creative ways as you further your own exploration of God's invitation to partnership.

Session 1
A New Definition of Partnership

Introduction

Begin with a brief overview of the genesis of pastoral partnership, previous workshops and learning opportunities that have been offered, and the vision for congregational participation.

Or begin by explaining why this is a concept your congregation wants to explore, where the impetus came from, and what the anticipated outcome is.

Defining Our Terms

Before this session, place each separate word of the partnership definition on paper or index cards. Use the definition in the paragraph below or your own definition of partnership. You will need one set of words for each small group.

Divide the group into smaller groups of three to five people. Give each group a set of the words that make up the definition of partnership. Ask the groups to put the words in the order that makes the most sense to them, based on what they know of the pastoral partnership they have experienced (or based on what they know about the potential partnership at this point). Ask each small group to share their version of the definition with the group. Talk about where they experienced clarity and where they got stuck.

On newsprint or white board, write the definition of partnership for the group to see: "A freely chosen, nonhierarchical relationship of mutual vision, power, and responsibility with equal commitments, risks, and rewards for the purpose of birthing new spiritual community."

Highlight the key vocabulary: nonhierarchical, mutuality, power, new spiritual community, and freely chosen. These words will be the focus of the next sessions.

Overview of the Eight Sessions

Each session will concentrate on one of these specific vocabulary terms in order to

- discover its roots in biblical imagery,
- understand its meaning and importance in the context of partnership,
- consider its implications for individual and communal ministry,
- envision its application for our church's organizational structure,
- discern its value among our church's communal values.

Biblical Beginnings—*The Church as the Body of Christ* (Ephesians 4:11–16; 1 Corinthians 12:4–31)

Scripture, and the New Testament in particular, provides many images for the church and our relationship to each other in faith: covenant, vine and branches, shepherd and sheep, household of God, city of God, New Jerusalem. Paul uses the imagery of the human body to visualize the relationship of persons and gifts to one another in the church. For centuries this has been a primary image for organizing congregational life.

Divide the whole group into two groups, asking each group take one of these passages: Ephesians 4:11–16 or 1 Corinthians 12:4–31. Invite them to respond to the questions below within their groups. Then share the findings of each group with the whole.

Questions related to the texts:

- In what ways has the church responded to and interpreted Paul's imagery? (For example, as a support for the priesthood of all believers, as justification for the ranking of gifts based on perceived importance, encouraging individual participation in and discernment of ministries.)
- What evidence, if any, of this image do you find in our congregational life?
- What is affirming about this imagery? What is troublesome about this image?
- What is missing from this image?

Body Sculpture

Invite each group to construct a visual depiction of their understanding of the body of Christ, using their own bodies. Encourage all to participate and then have the groups interpret their "sculpture" to each other. Notice similarities and differences.

Invitation

Invite the group to participate in this process of envisioning partnership with the following:

As the congregation and its leaders talk about partnership, we are inviting you to be a part of creating a new image for the church, not necessarily as a corrective to Paul's but as another way of looking at our life together in response to the movement of God's Spirit.

Observations, Hopes, and Questions

Invite participants to share new ideas, deeper appreciation, greater challenges, and resistance they have noticed, hopes they sense rising in themselves, and questions they have about partnership and its implications.

Session 2
Envisioning a Starting Place

Introduction

Recap the purpose of expanding a partnership vocabulary and deepening understanding about its possible implications for the church's communal life. You might say: "In the previous session we talked about the 'body of Christ' as Paul's imagery for the church. Today you will think about your own imagery for your experience at our church."

Imaging Our Faith Community

Encourage class members to design and create a visual image that represents the congregation's life and ministry as they experience it, taking into consideration its various ministries, how decisions are made, the role of leadership, and relationships.

Invite participants to play with a variety of media to complete their task—construction paper, cardboard, colored pens, markers, crayons, yarn, string, glue, staples, felt, Styrofoam, clay, Legos, or a junk box with miscellaneous items such as buttons, ribbons, paper clips.

For those who find building and creating with their hands uncomfortable, an alternative to arts and crafts might be an invitation to play with words. Participants could write an advertisement describing the church, a poem, a newspaper feature story; record a self-interview; or create a word search from a list that describes the church and their experience.

Reflection

Invite participants, one by one, to share their images, explaining what they created, either with things or words, and why.

Collect on newsprint some of the key elements that each contribution represents. Notice how people describe their experience of leadership and of relationships. What values are being communicated as a result of how leadership and relationships are experienced? What is being said about the use of power? Where do the individuals view themselves in their image of the church—for example, in the center, on the sideline, or somewhere in-between?

Display all the images for participants to see; consider leaving them in the room to be reflected on again.

Invitation

Share the following ideas with the group.

Expressing our experience of the church allows us to notice each other's starting place. Individual experience is important in partnership; we value what each brings to the conversation so that all might be challenged by it. In our society, one of the starting places for organizations like the church has been hierarchy. Next time we will look at hierarchy and the church and at what a nonhierarchical relationship like partnership might look like.

Observations, Hopes, and Questions

Invite participants to share things they have noticed, hopes they sense rising in themselves, and questions they have about partnership and its implications.

Session 3
A New Way of Relating

Introduction

All of us are familiar with hierarchy, although most of us are not aware of when it is operating. Because we are so accustomed to its presence and its corresponding set of values, we do not always notice hierarchy; we simply think, "That's the way life is." Hierarchy in the church is no different. Partnership, however, envisions relating in another way. Jesus's ministry offers us a very different perspective.

Biblical Beginnings—*Feeding the More Than 5,000* (Mark 6:30–44)

Read the passage aloud, taking turns around the group. Then allow each participant to choose a small group, either "Jesus," "disciples," or "crowd." Ask each group to pretend it is the character or characters selected (Jesus, the disciples, or the crowd). Provide each group with a handout containing the following questions to help them imagine themselves in the story:

> Where are you and what are you doing (sitting, standing, listening, talking)?
> Where are you in relationship to the others?
> What do you see?
> What are you feeling?
> What is the problem?
> How do you respond?
> Or not respond?
> How do you feel about it?

After each group has a sense of their part in the story, invite them to discuss these questions:

> What is the relationship between your character(s) and power?
> How is power used or not used?
> What is your intended outcome?
> What power shifts happen in the story?
> What does the experience of power in this story lead you to understand about power?

Give each group cutout symbols representing Jesus, the disciples, and the crowd (for example, a triangle for Jesus, a fish for the disciples, a chain of people for the crowd). Include two sets of several arrows each, one set with arrows that have a point on one end and another set with arrows that have points on both ends, perhaps different colors. With the symbols provided, ask the group to diagram power in the story from the position of the character(s) they have reflected on. Show how power is used, how it moves, what its results are. Ask each group to share their diagram and explain it to the entire group.

Partnership Vocabulary

Share the following ideas with participants:

In the definition of partnership used in this book, the phrase "nonhierarchical" is significant. Partnership is an intentional effort to offer a model of relating that is free from hierarchical assumptions about power, resources, and goals. Nonhierarchical relationships make the assumption that power is mutual, shared, and limitless. Nonhierarchical relationships experience a group's focal point shifting with the energy and movement of God's Spirit within the group. Nonhierarchical relationships value individual gifts, relationships, and experiences and view them as resources to be shared with the whole. The whole group shares responsibility, accountability, and commitment.

Reflection

Ask the entire group to respond to the following questions. Record their answers on newsprint:

What does Jesus's example in this text look more like—hierarchy or nonhierarchy? What specific things can you point to that indicate this?

What could be the implications of Jesus's example for our lives as individuals, leaders, and a faith community? What could these implications look like at our church?

Invitation

Share the following ideas with participants:

This biblical account is a key illustration of Jesus's value of a nonhierarchical, weblike way of relating. While hierarchy assumes that power and resources are limited, and therefore limits leadership, partnership assumes an abundance of all. By dividing the large group into smaller groups, Jesus invited the people to intimacy, mutuality, and abundance that came not out of his power, but out of their own.

Observations, Hopes, and Questions

Invite participants to share things they have noticed, hopes they sense rising in themselves, and questions they have about partnership and its implications.

Session 4
Mutuality

Introduction

Share the following summary with participants:

In the previous session we looked at Mark's version of Jesus's feeding the more than 5,000 as an example of a nonhierarchical, interdependent way of relating and leading, with *nonhierarchy* being the significant partnership vocabulary word. Today we will consider Jesus's invitation to mutuality.

Biblical Beginnings—*Redefining Greatness* (Luke 22:24–27)

Ask someone to read the text from Luke aloud for the class. Allow for a time of silence. Have a different person read the text again, perhaps from a different translation. Again, allow silence for reflection.

Invite participants to pair off. Ask each individual to respond to the following:

- The disciples were arguing over who was the greatest, who would be first. Have you ever been the first in or at something? What did that feel like? If you have not been first, when have you wanted to be the first, the best, the greatest? Why was that important to you? What were your hopes around that?
- Jesus says that to be first we must be last—that is, "one who serves." What does that image stir up for you? Describe a time when you have felt truly served by another. What was that like? How did it feel? If you can, describe a time when you have truly been a servant as Jesus suggests. What was that like?

Partnership Vocabulary

Share these ideas with the group:

Mutuality in partnership describes the nature of our relationships; it frames how we act and think about vision, power, and responsibility. Mutuality invites a level playing field, sharing, and deep respect. Each participant is valued equally; each voice is heard for the benefit of all.

Reflection

Ask the entire group to respond to the following questions. Record their answers on newsprint:

What do we usually desire when we want to be the greatest, like the disciples?

What do we usually fear when we think about being a servant?

What does Jesus's model say to us about our desires and our fears?

What would change about us and about our community if we truly embraced Jesus's vision?

Invitation

Share these ideas with the group:

Jesus inverts the hierarchal value system that causes us to rank one another and ourselves and instead goes to the heart of mutuality. That Jesus's model is not reflected or valued as normative in our society, any more than it was in his, is clear to us. Think of one concrete difference you would have to make in at least one relationship you participate in to reflect Jesus' value of mutuality.

Observations, Hopes, and Questions

Invite participants to share things they have noticed, hopes they sense rising in themselves, and questions they have about partnership and its implications.

Session 5
Playing with Power

Introduction

Share these ideas with the group:

"In the last two sessions we have looked at Jesus's feeding the more than 5,000 people as an example of Jesus's nonhierarchical, interdependent leadership style and at his invitation to the disciples to become those who serve as a model for mutuality. This week we will look at Jesus's reinterpretation of power in relationships.

Biblical Beginnings—*Called as Friends* (Matthew 23:1–12; John 15:12–17)

Ask the group to read these verses from the Gospels of Matthew and John aloud, taking turns around the room. Invite participants to choose at least one way to express their understanding of either text by doing one of the following:

- Write a pithy proverb that summarizes in a sentence what Jesus is trying to say in this text.
- Express your emotional, gut response to Jesus's words by shading those words with various colors (you determine the meaning of the color) on a copy of the text provided.
- Draw before and after pictures or diagrams of Jesus's teaching in one of these texts.
- Write a definition of the words *servant* (Matthew 23:1–12) and *friend* (John 15:12–17) based on what you understand Jesus to be saying.

Share participants' experiences of these texts with the whole group. Create a composite interpretation of each passage on newsprint, as people share their truths, feelings, visuals, and ideas.

Partnership Vocabulary

Share these ideas with the group:
Power is neutral; it is neither good nor bad. Power reflects the values of those who use it by the manner in which they use

it. In partnership, mutuality is the lens through which we look at power. In partnership, power is unlimited; it increases when shared; it is dominance free. In partnership, power is relational; it is collaborative, not competitive, and is exercised with mutual respect and recognition of others.

Reflection

Ask participants to think about these questions:

> What does our composite interpretation of the scripture passages have to say about power?
>
> What kind of power was present and active in Jesus's day?
>
> What vision for power does Jesus model for the disciples and for us?
>
> What would that power look like in relationships—at our church, in our families, among friends, even at work?

Invitation

Share these ideas with the group:

Jesus invites us to a discipleship of equals, a dominance-free relationship with each other and with him that is radically different than that of our (or his) societal norm. Partnership offers us a way of relating to each other that reflects Jesus's value of equality, mutuality, and respect. It takes seriously Jesus's words and invites us to change how we relate to each other.

Observations, Hopes, and Questions

Invite participants to share things they have noticed, hopes they sense rising in themselves, and questions they have about partnership and its implications.

Session 6
New Spiritual Community

Introduction

Share these ideas with the group:

In our previous sessions, we have thought about the terms *nonhierarchical, mutuality,* and *power,* looking at biblical underpinnings for a different way of relating. Today we will explore the importance of these relationships, because they open us to new spiritual community.

Biblical Beginnings—*Sharing a New Beginning* (Acts 10:1–11:18)

Because this is such a long Bible passage, instead of asking people to read it all, divide participants into small groups and invite each group to be responsible for one of the following sections:

> Acts 10:1–16
> Acts 10:17–29
> Acts 10:30–43
> Acts 10:44–48

Invite each group to present their portion of the story as a drama. Participants can act it out, having speaking parts or a narrator, or pantomime—whatever creative way they can tell their portion of the biblical text. Encourage them to work out how they pass off to the next group so that the story is told as seamlessly as possible. It is like round-robin storytelling that involves the entire group.

After the text is dramatized (be sure to fill in any significant gaps), summarize the conclusion in Acts 11:1–18 (in particular, read Peter's words in verses 15–17) and have the group consider this:

This story is about the experience of radical change, first in the life and experience of an individual, then a few more, and then in an entire group. Think of an experience of change like this that has happened to you or that you are aware of.

> What would it feel like to be Peter?
> What would it feel like to be Cornelius?
> What would it feel like to be the church at Jerusalem?
> What was at stake here?
> What were the potential losses and gains?
> Who or what was the agent of change?
> What was required for this change to take place?

Partnership Vocabulary

Share these ideas with the group:

Partnership opens up space—spiritually, structurally, relationally—for the creation and birth of new spiritual community, for a deeper expression and fuller understanding of God's Spirit, for healthier relationships, for new expression of God's presence in our midst. It invites us to create opportunities for new ways of relating to one another and to God. As we endeavor to envision what is yet to be, we open ourselves to God's invitation to see one another and ourselves in fresh ways and to allow ourselves to be moved and guided by God's Spirit in ways that both surprise us and give us life.

Reflection

Ask participants to consider the following questions:

> What parallels can be drawn between God's challenge and
>   change in the life of the early believers and in our own
>   lives?
> What would new spiritual community require?
> What might it involve?
> What might it look like?
> What are the risks?

Invitation

Share these ideas with the group:

Partnership in and of itself is not our goal but a way to move us toward new spiritual community. God's Spirit can only do something new in us if we are open to it. The change experienced by the early church led them into a deeper experience of God and each other. Are we also willing to be led?

Observations, Hopes, and Questions

Invite participants to share things they have noticed, hopes they sense rising in themselves, and questions they have about partnership and its implications.

Session 7
Freely Chosen

Introduction

Share these ideas with the group:

We have been working through some key phrases and ideas in the definition of *partnership*. One of the first phrases in the definition is "freely chosen." We have left this phrase for the end of our study, because, to make a meaningful choice, we need to have a deeper understanding of partnership.

Biblical Beginnings—*Freedom's Choice* (John 13:1–20)

Invite the group to read the text silently. Remind participants that making choices implies some degree of freedom; for there to be a real choice, there has to be an alternative.

Ask them to reflect on these questions:

What freedom is expressed in the text? What choices are made? What values are reflected in those choices?

List the values reflected by Jesus, Peter, and the other disciples.

In pairs, have the participants respond to the following:

Imagine that you were to place yourself in the story.
Where would you choose to be?
What would you see, hear, taste, smell, and feel from your
vantage point?
Describe where you are and what surrounds you.
What choices are you making?
What values do they represent?
What do you hear Jesus saying?
What is he saying to you?
What will be your response?

Partnership Vocabulary

Share these ideas with the group:

Saville Sax and Sandra Hollander, in *Reality Games: The Games People Ought to Play—A Way of Relating to Others with Greater Clarity, Directness and Depth,* use the term "complete value." For a value to be completely held, they suggest, it must be freely chosen from among alternatives after thoughtful consideration. The value should be something one feels good about and talks about publicly. It should be acted upon and evident in the pattern of one's life.[1]

Partnership must be freely chosen in this same way. It is a value to be lived, not just an idea to think about. When we intentionally choose partnership, we believe that we are choosing something much closer to Jesus's vision for God's reign than the church or our society has seen before.

Reflection

Ask the group to consider these ideas:

Jesus's values were reflected in his actions. He chose to relate to people in ways radically different from the societal norm because he envisioned God's reign, acted on it, talked about it, and made it the pattern of his life.

Can partnership be a chosen value for you, for your way of relating to others? If yes, what makes it possible for you to affirm it? If no, then what makes it difficult for you affirm it? Is it possible for partnership to become a "complete value" for our church? What would that look like? What would it mean for our life together?

Invitation

Share these ideas with the group:

We believe that Jesus offers us concrete examples, wisdom, and teaching for how to be in relationship with one another in ways that reject dominance, embrace mutuality, and usher in more fully the reign of God. We can make a choice about how we live individually and as a community of faith, inviting each other to be open to God's Spirit anew.

Observations, Hopes, and Questions

Invite participants to share things they have noticed, hopes they sense rising in themselves, and questions they have about partnership and its implications.

Session 8
Envisioning Something New

Introduction

Share these ideas with the group:

Over the course of this study, we have attempted to draw deeper meaning and understanding from our definition of partnership, the biblical text, and the wisdom of our own experience. Today you are invited to envision a new image of our community as partners.

Revisiting the Definition

Ask the group to reconstruct the definition of partnership (either the book's or another definition you created—whichever has been used through this study) as closely as possible from memory. Notice what is added to the definition and what is left out.

"Partnership is a freely chosen, nonhierarchical relationship of mutual vision, power, and responsibility with equal commitments, risks, and rewards for the purpose of birthing new spiritual community."

Ask the group to recall some images of the church that members of the group created in session 2 (if the images are still available show them; if not, just mention them). Note the shapes, sizes, symbols, and colors that people used.

A New Image

Share this idea with the group:

We envision the experience of partnership in community to be something like a web—not a spider's symmetrical web, but a web of interrelatedness that connects us to each other.

Next, invite the group to form one large, circlelike shape (as much as possible). You as facilitator begin with a ball of yarn (variegated rainbow yarn is nice) and, after securing it around a finger, toss it to someone else with whom you share a connection and naming the thing or person you have in common. For example, you might say: "I am connected to Karen because we serve on the Board of Christian Education together." Another might say: "I am connected with Tom because we both like golf." The recipient of the string wraps it around his or her finger, identifies a connection, and throws it to another person, and so on. Keep going until a multilayered web is formed.

With the web in place, reflect on these questions:

What do you notice about the web?

What is necessary for it to form and to stay in place?
What happens when someone drops his or her piece? (Carefully try it!)

Identify a specific group of people (those sitting near the door, for example) and invite the members of that group to pull gently on the web. What happens to the whole?
Identify a different group and pull again. What happens?
Discuss the following questions as a group:

What does the web suggest about power?
What does the web suggest about mutuality?
What does the web suggest about nonhierarchy?
What does the web suggest about new spiritual community?

Reflection

Ask group members to think about the following ideas and questions:
Partnership is like a web. It invites us to see each other and ourselves in a radically different way, to be open to new ways of relating, and to seek God's Spirit moving among us in life-giving ways. It is a transformative style of relationship that dares to embody a vision of the reign of God.
What would partnership look like at our church? What would have to change for us to move in that direction? What should be our next steps?
What might new spiritual community bring to our church? What might God be calling us to? What might be the risks? What might be the rewards?

Partners Together Lowering the Dowel

Ask the group to divide into smaller teams of about four to six people, and give each group a thin wooden dowel approximately one-half inch in diameter. Have half of each group stand on either side of the dowel facing the others. Ask people to hold out one hand, palm facing up, and extend the index finger. Gently place the dowel on the outstretched fingers and have the group hold it there. Now instruct the group to lower the dowel without touching it in any other way. Give them several minutes to work at the task before inviting them to reflect on the experience. After everyone has tried to lower the dowel, one team might observe another team to see what they can learn.

Together discuss what happened in each group:

What direction did the dowel go?
How did the group handle what happened?
What did you notice about power? About mutuality?
What made it work? Or not work?
What did you notice about relationships?

Invitation

Share these ideas with the group:

God's invitation to us in Christ is an invitation to a new way of relating, not only to God but also to one another. Rather than mirror the traditional, hierarchical models of the world, the church has the opportunity to demonstrate the radical, transfor mative nature of God in its relationships and structures. Such a demonstration requires openness to God's Spirit, a willingness to "think outside the box" about what we do and how we do it, and a desire to envision something new. We believe God is inviting us to a new way of being with each other and in the world, a way that deepens our connections to each other and also to our God.

Observations, Hopes, and Questions

Invite participants to share things they have noticed, hopes they sense rising in themselves, and questions they have about partnership and its implications.

Appendix B

Web Visions:

Leadership as Community

A Sermon Series

⌒◯This series of sermons was written and preached for the worshiping community of Central Baptist Church, Wayne, Pennsylvania. Not originally written for publication, they reflect the oral tradition of interpreting the Scriptures both in the context of the text and in our own time. The focus of Central Baptist's worship was exploring the image of the web as a way to describe the deepening sense of spiritual community that was resulting from partnership. The setting, described in chapter 4, included an enormous web created with rope and hung on the wall behind the preacher. Prayers, songs, biblical texts, and these sermons combined to remind us of the power of the Spirit's movement in our midst.

Knit Together

Marcus Pomeroy
Ephesians 4:1–7, 11–16 NRSV

I therefore, the prisoner in the Lord, beg you to lead a life worthy of the calling to which you have been called, with all humility and gentleness, with patience, bearing with one another in love, making every effort to maintain the unity of the Spirit in the bond of peace. There is one body and one Spirit, just as you were called to the one hope of your calling, one Lord, one faith, one baptism, one God and [Parent] of all, who is above all and through all and in all.

But each of us was given grace according to the measure of Christ's gift. . . . [And] the gifts he (Christ) gave were that some would be apostles, some prophets, some evangelists, some pastors and teachers, to equip the saints for the work of ministry, for building up the body of Christ, until all of us come to the unity of the faith and of the knowledge of the Son of God, to maturity, to the measure of the full stature of Christ. We must no longer be children, tossed to and fro and blown about by every word of doctrine, by people's trickery, by their craftiness in deceitful scheming. But speaking the truth in love, we must grow up in every way into him who is the head, into Christ, from whom the whole body, joined and knit together by every ligament with which it is equipped, as each part is working properly, promotes the body's growth in building itself up in love.

We are knit together, and that's not just a nice, feel-good idea. It is the kind of thing that you will sing about in church or you'll hear, maybe selling Coca-Cola—"I'd like to teach the world to sing." It's not just something that's a feel-good idea. It is an undeniable fact of reality. At the most basic level, there is no such thing as independence. You've heard it here today, in a Baptist church, for heaven's sake.

I say "at the most basic level" because if, for instance, all of the water was taken out of my body and there was just the dry weight here, 10 percent of what is left, 10 percent of that dry weight, is composed of bacteria. (But don't think about this, please, don't even imagine it.) Creation itself, starting with our own bodies, is composed of colonies of all kinds of things. Ten percent of me without the water, and some days there is more than others, but 10 percent of me is essentially alien life, but it's there. But it is not really alien because we've worked out this really nifty relationship, these bugs and me, most of the time.

There is a natural tendency for life to connect, to establish these mutually beneficial relationships, to form itself into living communities. Life does this because community is essentially a friendly thing to life. It makes it possible for life to be sustained much more creatively, and probably long term, than an individual life-form out there drifting around someplace. Communities provide, among other things, stability and support. An even more important byproduct, however, of community is freedom, because communal life actually increases the range of possibilities and makes it possible for each of us in our own way, and for the little bugs that are also part of us here this morning (we won't think about that though); all of those living realities, actually because of community, have more options available to them. So, actually, community increases freedom and possibilities. It fosters the individual experimentation that is so essential for life to continue to flourish.

The writer of Ephesians thousands of years ago knew all of this and was very much aware of the fact that community actually creates more possibilities in life—actually fosters this. The writer says diversity is a good thing, and therefore the Spirit has set it up so that there are some that are apostles, some that are prophets, some that are evangelists, some pastors and teachers to equip the saints for the work of ministry, for building up the body of Christ. We are knit together, connected in a community of relationships that fosters more life, more freedom, and more diversity. Over the next several weeks we will be exploring this web of relationships at Central Baptist Church and elsewhere. Specifically how, out of these colonies of life within our own community here, leadership has emerged. How these networks of relationships shape our communal life and give us freedom and more life. We are knit together as a community for mutual benefit, strength, freedom, possibilities.

The first thing I want us to notice is that this communion changes each one of us and is changed by us. If you would tweak this web up here [referring to the web on the wall behind him], so to speak, pull on it, you would notice that the whole thing begins to move around. That is the way it is with our community. Imagine for a second that there are lines, pieces of string that connect you with the people around you and maybe across the room. You don't have to be connected to everyone here with a line, because you're not; but there are relationships that are a part of those [other relationships that connect those who aren't directly connected]. So imagine just for a second that there is a line that is part of the relationship that you have with others in this communion. All of us are linked together. If you tug on the line, it begins to move the rest of us around. We each participate, you see, very really. This is not metaphor we're talking about, we're talking about real life. We each participate in the growth and the development and the nurture of our neighbor so that no one of us can set the tone or direction or the priorities of the others. We all participate in establishing the conditions for our communal life. If some one of us happens to take off and do something untoward—like say, "Well, let's light some incense in the midst of our worship commons" (which I did one Sunday morning), only to discover that there are those within our communion who are allergic to such smells—who actually have a physical reaction. Another example is our Communion bread. Say for instance that we start off assuming that we're all just the same and all just share Communion bread as though we all are just the same, not realizing that some of us have an allergic reaction to the wheat and the gluten that's part of our bread. You tug on the line anywhere and the rest of us begin to move. And we make adjustments and we make adaptations.

Let me give us some more examples. Some years ago— actually it's been about six or so—there were very few young people in our congregation. In fact, there were some of us who were very concerned. How do we get a youth group going? How do we attract young people? How do we attract families with young people? How do we involve ourselves in something with all of the issues that are part of the community of young people? Now there are going to be about 18 or 20 in our hot tub tonight. We have this growing, emerging, and wonderful group of young people that have, over the years, increased in number and activity and done all kinds of wonderful things as part of our communal life. This growth has influenced our community. We make decisions now with the understanding that we have to take seriously the young people in our midst. How can their lives be shaped in some sense and how can they shape our lives? Leadership needs, the allocation of time and space and money, all began with the growing number of children and youth in our community. You tug on it someplace and it begins to move around another place.

Another example: the realities and the concerns of the gay, lesbian, bisexual, and transgender persons in our community have shaped our life together. We have grown connected. It's not just an "us" and "them" type of thing. It's us! The realities of what we all experience are tied together, knit together in wonderful ways. What takes place with one of us does impact the others of us, all of us. And so, as a result, we have crafted a communal life that supports and nurtures and fosters more life for us all. When we celebrate anniversaries, we celebrate partners who have been together for 25 or 30 years, partners of the same gender, partners who are opposite genders. We have ordained people in our congregation, those who are straight but not narrow and those that are gay, lesbian, and bisexual, and transgender. Our communion has changed.

We have come to understand ourselves and the vision of what community—and particularly spiritual community—looks like. *This* is what it looks like! Gloriously, beautifully, wonderfully—this is what it looks like. And it makes it possible for all of us to be more human, more completely filled with the Spirit.

We are knit together. When one rejoices, all rejoice. When one suffers, all suffer. When we have members go to El Salvador and return, we're changed. All of us are changed. Not just those who went to El Salvador. But because of the change and transformation that comes back into this community and the way in which it feeds and nourishes us, it changes all of us.

When we invite Salvadoran brothers and sisters to visit us, we are changed. But we also change them, and we begin to change the reality of El Salvador, because we begin to catch a glimpse of each other's reality. And having seen, we'll never be the same again. We'll never be the same again. Every change, every place in the web of community changes other things, and strange though it may seem, this change, this process of change and emergence and growth is actually the way the web, the community, maintains its stability. If it didn't change, it would be torn apart, it would cease to be. It maintains its stability through these adaptations. In fact, the only way a community maintains stability is that change is taking place somewhere in the network of relationships. Somewhere along the line for it to maintain its integrity, there's got to be some change taking place that begins to manifest itself in the changes that are passed through the entire network.

That brings me to a second thing I want us to notice. That is, another word for stability is *identity*. A change actually makes it possible for the communal identity to be growing and pre-served. We're knit together in change to sustain our identity. Sounds weird, doesn't it? But it's true. Each of us then has a part to play—some apostles, some prophets, some evangelists, some pastors, some teachers, some whatever. For the purpose of equipping the saints, building up the body of Christ, the identity. Our identity as a community, a spiritual community, is as the body of Christ. We're knit together. That's who we are. And we change and adapt and evolve to sustain ourselves as the body of Christ; God with us, full of grace and truth, friend of the poor and the outcast.

Right from the get-go, Central Baptist Church came together around its identity as the body of Christ, and it wasn't just any old vision of this body that pulled this entire web together, all of these relationships. It was the Christ who liberated the oppressed, healed the afflicted, and welcomed the outcast. We emerged as a community over a hundred years ago in response to the scourge of slavery and became a living, growing communion whose identity was the Christ who set the captives free. That's the identity. And all of the changes and the growth and adjustments since have been to sustain this identity as the body of Christ, this body of Christ, this liberating body of Christ. This is who we are. And in a powerful way this community has chosen each one of us as much as we have chosen it. This community with its own life and its own power and its own sustaining resources, its own vision of identity as the body of Christ, as liberating power, has actually in some sense chosen you to be part of it. To be part of the network. To be part of the communion that sustains and changes. Each of us, you see, has been called. The Spirit has given us one another to equip the saints and build up the body. We are knit together. We change this communion and we are changed by this communion for the equipping of the saints, for the building up of the body of Christ.

I'm going to take us a step forward, or a step beyond maybe. I want to take the top of your head off for just a bit. Take the sides out of the church, the roof, for just a second. Because sometimes I think we limit ourselves, limit ourselves to too small a vision. We are a community that's knit together, but we are also a community in a vast network of communities. Not only within spiritual communities, but we're [also] connected with the educational community, with the local and state and national and international government communities. We are connected with the American Baptist Churches USA as well as the World Council of Churches and the National Council of Churches and all of the other churches. We are connected with all of the various faith communities of the world. We've come to be so deeply aware of how connected we are with the Islamic community. We are connected with the PBA, the Philadelphia Baptist Association. All of these communities. We are a community of communities, changing and adapting and being changed by that web as well.

Just as there is this bunch of bacteria taking up residence with me and we've worked out this wonderful partnership for each other's benefits, and just as we are a communion of saints to build up the body of Christ and each of us in some sense has been chosen and called to be a part of this communion, so this communion here, this community, is chosen as much as it chooses. It's called to be a spiritual community in the expanse of the universe. Called to be a spiritual community in relationship to the people of El Salvador, the people of India, the people of Burma, the people of England, the people of Alabama. We are a community called to be connected, to build up the body of Christ.

And here's the kicker—we can change the universe. We can change the universe! And can it be that the universe has actually called us into being us, into being as a spiritual community so that it might maintain its identity? Its life? Its integrity? Its communion? We are knit together. Thanks be to God.

Leading with Your Heart

Marcia B. Bailey
Luke 22:24–27 NRSV

> A dispute also arose among them as to which one of them was to be regarded as the greatest. But he said to them, "The kings of the Gentiles lord it over them; and those in authority over them are called benefactors. But not so with you; rather the greatest among you must become like the youngest, and the leader like one who serves. For who is greater, the one who

is at the table or the one who serves? Is it not the one at the table? But I am among you as one who serves."

The slogan used in advertising the doctor of ministry program at Colgate Rochester Crozer Divinity School when I began in 2001 was "a doctoral program for those who cannot leave well enough alone." It strikes me, after once again being in the company of those who have responded to this slogan out of a sense of *call,* some experiencing it as a challenge, and others as a liberation, that indeed Jesus might have been very much at home at CRCDS, a reality for which I am most grateful.

Certainly Jesus did not "leave well enough alone" throughout his life and ministry, and this dinner-table conversation is one more example. Most likely during a lull in the progression of the evening, the disciples begin to pick at each other: wrangling back and forth about who was going to have the biggest church, drive the flashiest car, raise the largest mission budget, have the most members on Easter Sunday morning. And like he did time and time before, Jesus interrupted their nonsense, reminded them of the way it was, and invited them to imagine something new.

It *is good* to be reminded of the way things really are; it's so easy to be blind to all the things we'd rather not see. Jesus's words brought to the disciples' minds the reality of the table—the long, rectangular, boardroom-like table, the seats around which each held a predetermined weight of authority. Those with the most money, the most power, the most honor, the most _____ (you fill in the blank) got to sit closest to the "top." Who would have ever guessed it? And you know where those with the least sat—right where they still sit today. Those with power wielded it and those with money paid for it. It's a system that seems to have worked, if not for all, then at least for some.

On Wednesday morning of this past week I presented the first draft of my thesis proposal to my colleagues, a frightening and exhilarating thing. As I shared our congregational vision for leadership as partners, for mutuality, interconnectedness—this

web—I was aware of one who was clearly uncomfortable, vis-
ibility agitated, shifting and sliding in her seat. During the ensu-
ing grilling (not really), she jumped into the dialogue with both
feet, stating, "I've just never *seen* anything like this. I don't *know*
anyone like this Marcus fellow (how true!) nor have I ever seen
anything like this ministry that you describe. It can't be *real!* I
don't think it exists."

It can't be real. Doesn't exist. She just couldn't imagine it, a
testimony to the strength of the reality of the "the way things
are."

Fortunately, even as her brokenness and longing was revealed,
the question of my integrity was dismissed as an old friend of
Ron and Betsy's, Bill Dean, looked at me and said, "This is the
most exciting thing I've ever heard imagined."

"Let the greatest among you become the follower," Jesus
reenvisions. Sure, it's *not* the way we always do it. But I dare
you to imagine a whole new thing.

Imagine relationships that are based on deep respect for each
person, where every single one is honored for who and what
they are. Imagine not leveling the playing field but inventing a
whole new game. Where those who have lived lifetimes on the
sidelines get to make the rules and call the plays and everybody
wins. Imagine sharing not out of wealth but out of poverty, not
out of guilt but out of grace. Imagine that the most significant
one at the celebration clears the table; that the stranger in our
midst becomes the host.

Imagine that, and you might begin to know something of the
invitation Jesus calls us to in our relationships with one another,
an invitation to subvert the reality of what is for what might be;
an invitation to honor and love and celebrate each other that
requires that we give and receive something new. Imagine a
mutuality that grows out of and into community—look around
you. Imagine that!

What Jesus was doing was reordering the nature of our
relationships with one another. Dispensing with the conven-

tional system of ranking—a system that labels and divides, that minimizes and disrespects—Jesus transforms what was into a new community marked by its love and service, its diversity and strength. Now, instead of an endlessly long table, it is this interconnected web that shapes our relationships and visions.

At a meeting last fall Marcus and I invited members of our Cabinet to form a web with rainbow-colored yarn marking their relationships with one another. Back and forth, around and across the circle the multicolored web wove movement and light, color and texture into a strong and delicate interconnected reflection of life and meaning. As each one held her or his piece, the multilayered web grew: flexible and accommodating, yet insistent and accountable. We discovered that when someone let go or dropped the piece of the web they were holding, the effect was noticeable but the web didn't fall apart. Those strands that were underneath supported those there were across the top; those that were in the middle held those that were at the sides. Mutuality in relationship invites us to imagine ourselves as weavers of this web, bright with our own colors yet held together in a strong and tender relationship that has life and shape and movement of its very own.

Mutuality invites us to see ourselves and one another seated around Jesus's dinner table, where laughter and love are plentiful, where there is more than enough for all to eat, where there is a place for everyone—*God makes a place,* where each one serves the other in humility and grace.

I told you about the woman who didn't think such a vision was possible; well there's more to the story, as you might have guessed. One by one we went around the table—in no particular order; there was no "head," no "foot." Each one gave voice to the vision for life and ministry that had brought them to that place; each one received the challenges and affirmations of the others, offered and returned in a spirit of mutuality and grace. And in those moments, the imagination of God's Spirit altered reality; leadership *was* in community, diversity celebrated, a vision of a new table set. But the woman who couldn't imagine it never did see it; she had already left.

The vision of the web is to imagine the new things God invites us to, to transform reality as we know it, to live in relationships that are life giving and new. Mutuality is not a thing to have but a way to be, a spirit that modifies everything we do: what we say and don't say to one another; how we speak and how we listen; what we do and choose not to do in community, in friendship, in faith. Jesus knew how things were and surprised them all by imagining something new—leadership with heart, community with grace. I am so pleased to walk in the company of others who can't "leave well enough alone," community that envisions a new reality in faithfulness to the living Christ—you!

The Inviting Spirit

Marcus Pomeroy
Acts 10:1–11:18 NRSV (selected verses)
(Instead of reading these two entire chapters of the book of Acts in worship, Marcus retold the biblical story.)

Cornelius was a centurion in Caesarea and a very important military commander, part of the occupation armies of the Roman Empire in Israel. There is some understanding that there are a couple of chapters in the book of Acts that have gotten rearranged over the course of the years, so that Peter's imprisonment, told a little bit later in the book of Acts, may have actually occurred before this story. So perhaps in that understanding, Cornelius would have known of Peter because he would have been part of the imprisoning powers.

Cornelius has a vision. He was praying, and in this vision he experiences a visitation by a heavenly being; the text says an angel. It could be any heavenly creature that might be in

Cornelius's spiritual experience. It is very interesting that what Cornelius experiences in this connectedness is an affirmation. "Cornelius, you're A-OK. Way to go! God has actually heard your prayers and God is very pleased by the way that you are sharing something of your generosity with the people that are poor, doing all kinds of things. Right on! Way to go, Cornelius." There is a sense of being in the right place, doing the right thing.

There is a sense of being centered, of being connected to that which is the best and good and right, of life. And in that affirmation, Cornelius experiences himself really alive, fully alive, fully himself. In this vision, then, he is instructed, or experiences himself led, to get in touch with this guy who was in prison under his authority—Peter—and to talk with him, hear what he's got to say. It doesn't say what he's got to say; [it] just says, "Go find Peter and listen." He doesn't have a clue really what he is going to hear.

In the meantime, Peter, in some other location, has gone onto the roof around noontime to have lunch, or wanting to have lunch; he was getting hungry. So while the meal was being prepared, it says that he falls into a trance. I have experienced that, others have experienced that, and sometimes you experience that in a sermon. Sometimes you experience that driving down the turnpike. More often than not, this is a spiritual experience; this is a deep relatedness to the Holy, to God, to that which is the ground of our life.

In this trance Peter sees a vision, and in this vision there is this sheet, this humongous sheet that is being lowered from the heavens by the four corners. When it gets low enough, what Peter sees on this sheet are all kinds of creatures. There are animals: snakes, lizards, turtles, and birds of various kinds. And then Peter hears in his inner voice a message that says, "Eat up. Take whatever you want and have it for lunch. You want surf and turf, you want fish and fowl, or whatever it is." Peter says, "Whoa, I can't do that. There's some stuff on there that the Law says I can't have. I've got certain scruples, religious scruples, you

understand. I don't eat just anything because I'm a pretty good
Jew." And then the voice of God says, "Hey, don't worry about
it. I've taken care of it. It's all been made right, clean. What I've
made right, don't worry about, Peter; it's right. Trust me."

Well, after awhile Peter woke up. I guess maybe lunch did
arrive. He was trying to figure this out. He couldn't quite understand what was going on. And while he was thinking about
this, the messengers from Cornelius come and say, "Hey, we're
looking for Peter." And so the word gets to Peter and they said,
"We've been sent here. You're to come with us." So Peter says,
"Come on in, we'll have some supper, and we'll go the next
day." So they head off. Peter doesn't have a clue why he is going.
Doesn't have a clue.

So when he gets there, Cornelius recounts to him his vision.
He says, "Here is why I sent for you, because I was told to send
for you." Peter then begins to say, "Well, you know, I had a vision too, and in this vision it was OK for me to come in and sit
down with you. Ordinarily, I wouldn't be here talking with you
because you're part of the occupation army and you're a Gentile;
you're not a Jewish person. I'm not supposed to sit here. There
are a whole bunch of things that are problematic." Cornelius
responds, "Shhh. Be quiet, Peter. God says it's all right, so it's
all right." Then Peter begins to tell about Jesus, who Jesus is.

When he gets finished with this, Cornelius and everybody
else that's there experience themselves enwrapped by God. Filled
with the Holy Spirit is the way it's talked about. And Peter says,
"Wow, look at this. God's in these Gentiles. How can this be?"
Then he says, "Let's baptize them because it is very evident that
this is God's presence here among us." What happened is that
Cornelius recognized that the one he had been experiencing in
his vision was the one that Peter gave a name to—Jesus. And
what Peter recognized was that Jesus is the one that was active
over here in Cornelius.

When the church in Jerusalem heard about this—and it
was kind of out of the ordinary, out of the box—they invited

Peter to come and give an accounting of himself, and when he finished telling the story, the church leaders said nothing. They were speechless. (This is a pivotal story in the book of Acts, and really it is a pivotal story in our history as a community of faith, as the church, because it really changed the face of the Jesus movement. Up until this time it was essentially and exclusively something that was coming to the people of Israel. It was a Jewish sect, so to speak. Here, all of a sudden, there is this story that is right in the center of all this activity that says, "Boom! This story of Jesus, this movement of the Spirit isn't just confined to the people of Israel. It's for everybody." It shows up a little bit later in the book of Acts as well.)

The only way that you and I, I think, can get a sense of how profound this whole thing was for Peter and the early church is to imagine for a second that the pope and Billy Graham and Anne Lamott and the Archbishop of Canterbury and Virginia Mollencott and Phyllis Tribble and maybe Desmond Tutu, all over the world, each one of them individually calls a press conference unbeknownst to the others. They say, "We've got some news to announce to you! Two thousand years of religious division are over. Jews and Christians are children of God and there's really no difference in God's sight, and we're all one big happy family, and we've got that on good authority. So now, hey, it's all over." I think that there would be some changes, perhaps, at the top. This kind of movement, you see, can only take place as a consequence of something that was so profoundly real that it couldn't, in some sense, be challenged.

The only way I think that we can understand this is that it is a movement of the Holy Spirit; it's the leadership of the Spirit. And what we are describing in this series on web visions is that this inviting Spirit, this one that was operating in Cornelius, it was operating in Peter, it was operating in whomever, this inviting Spirit really emerges out of the relationship, this network of relationships that is the people God is working with. Cornelius had a vision over here in Caesarea. Peter had a dream over here—I think it was in Joppa. Neither one of them knew what was going on. Each of them independently experienced some confusion, some doubt, some leadership, some kind of invitation and whatever. And it wasn't until they got together that they realized each of them had a piece of a puzzle and that, when they came together, the puzzle pieces fit.

Now you've got to admit that this is messy business. Sort of hit and miss, I think, a bit. It is unpredictable. Who knows whether or not Peter was going to actually follow the invitation. Who knows whether Cornelius was going to send off the messengers. But the outcome, you see, is spectacular. It's messy, but wow! Who would have thought that this could have taken place?

I had an interesting conversation a few weeks ago with Claudia Echavarria. Claudia gave me, in the course of this conversation, an image that is really a way of understanding the work of the Spirit. Claudia is a sculptor; she works in clay. Her sculptures have wonderful movement about them. They are very interesting designs, and it's just fascinating to see how she has created, out of her own sense of spirit and movement and creativity and vision, these pieces of work, of art. Nancy, [Marcus's wife] in wonderful love and affection, gave me a gift at Christmastime, a gift of one of Claudia's pieces. Claudia, in her wonderful gift, said, "You come and pick it out, whatever it is. We won't say it's just one thing. Come visit and see what I've got here in the process." So Nance and I went out there to see Claudia and Sally. And Claudia showed me the shop, and we were talking about the various pieces. I saw one that I liked, and she said, "Well, pick out maybe one or two others just in case something happens in the firing." So I picked out a couple of other pieces that maybe would work OK.

She talked about the firing and she showed me a piece that had been in this kiln where it had been fired to an incredible temperature, and it shimmered. The surface absolutely was translucent. It was fascinating. It was alive. It was so cool. But

then she said, "You know, you might want to think about having it fired, not in this electric kiln, but maybe in a wood kiln.
Have it fired in this wood kiln." Then she showed me another
piece that had been fired in the wood kiln, and this one had all
kinds of wonderful designs and color and interesting movements.
And she says, "You know, the thing about firing in a wood kiln
is that it's absolutely unpredictable how it is going to come out
of there because there are all kinds of things that are variables.
It makes a difference as to what kind of wood is used; the ash
as it falls will color the piece in a different way, the atmospheric
condition, the barometer, the humidity, the temperature, the
person that fires the kiln, the wind conditions. All of these will
make a difference in the way the piece comes out of the kiln. In
fact, you can put two pieces in the same kiln and they'll come
out looking different because of this wonderful unpredictability."
But the results were spectacular! All of these things working, but
working in a way that was totally fresh, creative, new.

I thought about this in terms of the way that the Spirit is
actually working in our midst, and here for Cornelius, and here
for Peter. The way the Spirit works in relationship is that we really
don't know how it will turn out until it does. So, consequently,
it is important for us, if we are to be a community led by the
Spirit and to experience ourselves, in some sense, listening to the
Spirit's movements among our relationships, to constantly be
attentive. You can't just head off with a blueprint. It's constantly
following a presence and a reality and being in relationship with
the power and the Spirit that is among us. We don't know where
it is going to show up next. It could be in the ash that filters
down; it could be in the wind that blows along; it could be in
the person who is stoking the fire. It is messy and unpredictable,
this business of being led by the Spirit.

But there are, nevertheless, some guidelines, and we learn
some of these from looking at what happened with Cornelius
and Peter. Actually, I want to say that Ignatius lifted all of this
stuff out in one way or another, and said, "Pay attention. This

is the way you follow the Spirit. Pay attention to the beginning, the middle, and the end. It may start off over here and you may assume that you've got it all scoped out. But you need to pay attention to the way it moves, this Spirit, through the middle and through the end. Because, unless you follow the Spirit all the way, you're not going to end up where the Spirit is leading."

First, Cornelius paid attention and followed and Peter paid attention and followed. They discovered in this following that the Spirit actually was coming to meet them. It's not enough for you just to individually experience yourself being called by God. There needs to be some confirmation out there that God is calling from over there. As you move along, you need to notice whether or not you're coming closer to God. Is the Spirit coming to meet you? Is there an invitation? It may be strong; it may be weak; it may be hardly a whisper; but is there something that tugs at the corners of your heart? It is important then to pay attention to that and to follow. And as we follow, to notice whether or not we encounter the Spirit coming toward us.

The second thing: pay attention to the beginning, pay attention to the center. Do we recognize Jesus in this encounter? As we move along encountering this energy, this life, this person, this relationship, do we recognize Jesus in that relationship? Do we experience, as we follow, a growing awareness that this is God's presence? Cornelius, you remember, recognized in what Peter was saying that this is the one that Cornelius had known; now he had a name for that One. Peter similarly recognized in Cornelius that this is the one that he had known. Unlike Peter, Cornelius didn't have a name for it. The middle, the end. Does the invitation, as we follow, build community? Are more connections made? Is communion created? Are relationships formed? Does justice begin to happen? Does reconciliation begin to be experienced? Do we find ourselves closer and closer, knit together as people of faith?

I'm going to hold up four things from our communion here just for us to look at with these things in mind: Is there an invitation? Do we meet the Spirit as we move along? Do we recognize Jesus? Does it build community? There are some things that are tugging at us.

Over the last some months, our Board of Outreach and others have been wrestling with the questions around our relationship with Ruth and Alex Orantes. Ruth and Alex, as you remember, visited us some years ago. They are wonderful, beautifully creative, powerfully motivated people of faith who have been teaching at the seminary in El Salvador, leading churches and working among the poor, seeking justice and rebuilding after the hurricane, rebuilding after the earthquake, and doing all kinds of things to bring about some sense of new life within the people in the community of El Salvador. But the reality is that, as is often the case with creative people, they don't quite fit into institutional structures. They get jammed by them, so that the institutional structures, when they get people that don't quite fit in, they boot them out. So Alex, as he's been leading and following the Spirit, has been booted out of several places, and the last place was the Federation of Baptists in El Salvador. We have prayed about what we do, in response to this long-standing relationship, to this sense in which our heart is tugged by Ruth and Alex. How can we as Central Baptist Church in some sense respond to make it possible for Alex's and Ruth's gifts to be available to the community of faith? We went over and talked with Stan Slade at International Ministries [Board of International Ministries, American Baptist Churches USA]. We talked to Sara Stowell who is with the SHARE Foundation to see if she would be able to work with Alex and Ruth. We were cautious because we didn't want to establish [a] relationship that would set them up for rejection by other Baptist leaders. We were cautious because we didn't want to develop a dependency that was going to be long standing. We began then to ask ourselves, to ask ourselves the question—and I ask you this morning, as we listen together around this question of what are we to do in relationship to these partners—do we experience the Spirit meeting us as we follow this invitation? What do we recognize as we go in relationship with Ruth and Alex? Do we recognize Jesus there? Do we experience a growing sense of communion and community and connectedness?

Another example: after the tragic events of September 11, [2001,] and the equally tragic events of death and destruction in the months that have followed as a consequence of the bombing, the terrible assault on the people of Afghanistan—not just the Taliban, but the people of Afghanistan—several of our members, led by Andy Smith, experienced an invitation by the Spirit to establish some connections with the Islamic Society of Greater Valley Forge [Pennsylvania]. The invitation was, first of all, to get to know these neighbors and friends, to understand something about the Islamic faith, [to] begin to build some community bridges between us, and to accompany one another in a hostile environment. In these conversations, we met Ajmal Khan and Nassar Khan, and we prayed together with the community; some of us did. We've developed, as a consequence of this invitation, some movement to continue conversations, and I ask the question again for all of us to discern.

Do we experience the Spirit meeting us as we go down this road? The Spirit. Do we recognize Jesus as we enter into these conversations as we meet one another? Do we notice the creation of community as a consequence of these conversations, these relationships?

One more example: over the past few months we have been engaged in conversation around worship and music. We've discovered, to no one's surprise, that we are a diverse community. We have different interests and desires for music and worship. Different things satisfy us. On any different Sunday it could be one thing or it could be another thing. I was having lunch with a friend and several other people who are not members of Central Baptist. This friend happens to be on our mailing list and was laughing in front of these other people saying, "Central Baptist

Church is so unusual, so unique in so many different ways, but there, all across the newsletter, is this article about the church having these conversations about music. They're just like every other Baptist church I've ever known." I was a little embarrassed. We've expended a fair amount of time and energy in this conversation. So I'm going to ask these questions of discernment. Do we experience the Spirit inviting us into these conversations? Do we experience the Spirit meeting us as we go into this? Do we recognize Jesus in these conversations with one another and in this back and forth? And do we notice the creation and the building up of community as we go down this line?

We're meeting as a congregation following this worship service. There have been some tough discernments and struggle around budget and there have been some honest and very sincere differences that we face as a community about what we're going to do together. I invite you, as we meet around the tables and as we begin to talk with one another, to hold these questions in your minds. Watch where we experience Spirit coming to meet us. We'll know that because we'll begin to notice something about love and joy and peace and patience and kindness and self-control. These are the gifts of the Spirit. If we experience some of that, then we can say, "OK, let's keep going in this direction."

Notice where we recognize Jesus in one another. I'm not talking about the plastic Jesus; I'm talking about the Jesus of justice, the Jesus of peace and reconciliation, the Jesus of truth, the Jesus who is able to side with the oppressed, the Jesus that brings healing and wholeness, the Jesus that liberates us from our oppressions and liberates us from the hatred and fears and concerns that we have about one another and ourselves. That's the Jesus that we need to recognize. Finally, let's follow those movements of the inviting Spirit that build community. Out of the kiln of the Spirit, the Spirit's fire, who knows what beautiful creation will emerge? Amen.

A + B = FEAST

Marcia B. Bailey and Marcus Pomeroy
Mark 6:30–44 NRSV

The apostles gathered around Jesus, and told him all they had done and taught. He said to them, "Come away to a deserted place all by yourselves and rest a while." For many were coming and going, and they had no leisure even to eat. And they went away in the boat to a deserted place by themselves. Now many saw them going and recognized them, and they hurried there on foot from all the towns and arrived ahead of them. As he went ashore, he saw a great crowd; and he had compassion for them, because they were like sheep without a shepherd; and he began to teach them many things. When it grew late, his disciples came to him and said, "This is a deserted place, and the hour is now very late; send them away so that they may go into the surrounding country and villages and buy something for themselves to eat." But he answered them, "You give them something to eat." They said to him, "Are we to go and buy two hundred denarii worth of bread, and give it to them to eat?" And he said to them, "How many loaves have you? Go and see." When they had found out, they said, "Five, and two fish." Then he ordered them to get all the people to sit down in groups on the green grass. So they sat down in groups of hundreds and of fifties. Taking the five loaves and the two fish, he looked up to heaven, and blessed and broke the loaves, and gave them to his disciples to set before the people; and he divided the two fish among them all. And all ate and were filled; and they took up twelve baskets full of broken pieces and of the fish. Those who had eaten the loaves numbered five thousand men.

Marcia: It was six years ago in January [1996] that you [Marcus] and I made a commitment to each other to follow a vision, to respond to an invitation, to dare to dance with a new Spirit as we discovered together what we might look like—what community might look like, what partnership might look like, what this interweaving of our relationships might look like in a way that was life giving, dynamic, and new.

Marcus: It was a dream I think that was born in this community, which emerged out of who we are and what we have been about. But it was a dream that had very little substance to it, as I recall. It was a dream that was as much hope as it was anything else. We had *some* pieces of the puzzle, but we didn't know how it went together at all. And what we realized was that it was one vision among many.

There were all kinds of ways we could put together a community of partnership, not only of pastoral partnership but [also] a community of partnership, recognizing that there are a number of different options and visions, but that this is one of them. As we began to work on this, we began to dig deeply into the Scriptures, our faith experience, and our communal life, as well, to find the spiritual, theological, and biblical resources out of which we could fashion this vision of what it would look like to be a community that was not hierarchical but was mutually respectful, seeking, in some sense, to give birth to new spiritual community. It was that which brought us to this series, and to some of the Scriptures that we've looked at over the course of these last several weeks. This particular Scripture this morning is one that has fed us as we thought together about building this partnership, this ministry of community leadership.

Marcia: We thought we'd share some of that feeding with you and invite you to chew on it as well, as together we think about this invitation that Jesus gives in this text but also has given among us. You see it's there. We may have not known it six years ago, but it's there. It's there in Mark's Gospel; it's there in all four of the Gospels that tell this story in all kinds of ways.

About Jesus and the disciples, about all these people, and [about] how it was that all of them were fed. It starts with the disciples coming to Jesus, but there's actually a piece that goes before it.

Marcus: Yes, and if you know your Scriptures, there [are] different places in the text where this actually shows up. What happened was that Jesus sent the disciples off on a mission trip—their first mission trip. He sent them out two by two and said, "Don't take very much with you. Find the resources that you'll be able to use within the communities that you experience; don't worry about the fact that you've just got your sandals and maybe a crust of bread. Look to the Spirit to guide you, and look for the Spirit within the communities you come to." They did. They went out there on this faith mission and they came back, and here's Jesus standing there waiting to greet them! And they're almost like kids, like getting home from school, saying, "Wow, baby, you won't believe what happened. It actually works!"

Marcia: I don't think they thought it *would* actually work. But it did. They healed people, they cast out demons, and they transformed lives. It worked. It *worked!* And there's Jesus standing there, and they're all grouped around him, saying, "You'll never believe what we did. I couldn't believe it myself," giving a testimony to each other's experiences about all this stuff that had happened. And Jesus, can you see him? He's excited, maybe there's this bemused look on his face, and he's thrilled with them. But he also sees more than what they see. (He always sees more than what they see.) So he invites them to come away. He says, "Let's have a little time out, guys—a little R & R, a little trip to Mexico. . . ."

Marcus: [Leaving for Mexico later that day] You just *had* to say that.

Marcia: I just *had* to get that in there. He invites them to come away to have an opportunity to reflect on what it is that's happened, about what's going on, and about who actually did this marvelous thing among them. So he invites them to come to the other side of the lake.

Marcus: Then Jesus saw the Spirit leading them into this renewal, recognizing that there is a pace involved in this ministry, that there's engagement, and then there's the movement back for refreshment. That there is the opportunity for us to give, but there's always the real important opportunity for us to receive. And that we do need to find ourselves in this movement back and forth, because it's so easy in the excitement of ministry to just give and give and fail to notice the reality that we've got to be replenished. It is the Spirit that provides this nourishment. So Jesus said, "OK, let's go."

What happens is that they get on the other side of the lake only to discover that here's this enormous crowd, and they [the crowd] could see them [Jesus and the disciples] as they're rowing up to the shore. They're coming in across the hillside. "Oh, gee, what's going to happen? Some vacation."

Marcia: Like if we go *with* you to Mexico!

Marcus: What happens is that Jesus begins to experience the Spirit actually leading in a different direction at this point. He sees this community that is gathering there on the hillside, on the shore of the lake, and recognizes that they are a community that is hungry, a community that needs to be fed, a community that's bringing its own emptiness here. Instead of the Spirit, in some sense, inviting them to go off into this solitude and refreshment, it is actually the Spirit that has changed direction. Jesus is very sensitive and begins to feed them, teach them.

Marcia: I imagine at this point that the disciples are around the periphery, letting Jesus do his thing. And Jesus goes on and on and on. Jesus continues to teach, and there's this energy that goes between Jesus and this crowd, and yet the disciples are there checking their sundials and noticing that it's getting later. They begin to see the crowd and the need that these people have. Yes, they need to hear what Jesus has to offer them, but they also have some very real physical needs too. And so the disciples, maybe cognizant of their own need around this too, give Jesus the signal for time out.

Marcus: "Hear the grumbling? That's my stomach. It's getting late. Time to stop." So they come to Jesus and say, "Hey, we have a problem. These people are hungry. There's nothing around here to feed them. There's no Taco Bell; there's nothing. You don't see any hamburger stands, anything around close. Send these folks away." They saw the problem very clearly, and there was a real sense in which they were sensitive to the problem, but they jumped to a solution right off the bat. Here's the problem; we're going to solve it: send them [the people] out into the villages around so that they can find something to eat.

Marcia: That probably would be the most expedient and obvious choice. But, again, they saw it as a *problem,* and then they saw from their own resources, or lack thereof, that there was but one solution. This is all we *can* do. We have nothing. They have to go. Jesus, on the other hand, takes a different look at it, and his response is, "Well, *you* feed them. You feed them."

Marcus: Again, we experience Jesus watching very, very carefully the movement of the Spirit here. It's almost as if Jesus's eyes are focused not only on what is there but also on what's *there* (if you know what I mean).

Marcia: Like, there's more there than they can see, than they know about. "You feed them." So they object, of course. "It's going to take almost a year's wages! We don't have this kind of money. There's no grocery store; what are we going to do? We can't do this." So Jesus says, "How much bread have you got?"

They rummage around and, between the bunch of them, they've got five loaves. Somebody says, "Uh, I snagged two fish on the way over." I assume they think he's going to say, "Oh, you're right. We can't do this. Let's go. Everybody out of here." But he doesn't.

Marcus: Jesus redirected their vision from the *problem* to the *resources*. He says, "Look at yourselves, first of all. What you're looking at out there is scarcity. But look at yourselves first and notice what it is that you have as a person, as an individual, and as a community. Notice the connections between you. Notice what happens when, all of a sudden—instead of starting to look and get hung up out there in terms of this great, enormous problem, all of these hungry folks—what happens when you look in here. It's all here."

Marcia: The problem becomes *opportunity.* What can we do with this? What do we do? This is the reality. The other interesting piece is he not only gets them to look at their own resources, but he [also] gets them to look at who this crowd was. Mark says that Jesus doesn't do this. *Jesus* doesn't. They, *the disciples,* divide the crowds into smaller groups. But Jesus doesn't do that. Jesus instructs and empowers the disciples. He says, "Get them into smaller groups. Get this massive, faceless crowd into communities."

Marcus: And when they do, what happens is that the faceless become faced, in some sense. The people all of a sudden begin to experience themselves not so much as an anonymous group but as people who can see each other's eyes, hear each other's voices, sense each other's warmth of body and movement. It's not like they are there alone in a crowd, but they are there as a *community* of people, a small community of people, within this larger context.

We don't know what happens at this point. The Scriptures are the interpretation of what was remembered. What was

remembered is that *scarcity* became *abundance.* Five loaves and
two fishes ended up feeding everybody, or so it seemed.

Marcia: With some leftover, we're told. So then how did it
happen? I don't know, but I imagine that they took those loaves
and broke them into little pieces and said, "OK, you take this
bit and you take this one and you and you." And they began to
share those around those circles. I imagine that now, instead of
a crowd, this *community* looked at each other and said, "Well,
you know, I've got this," and someone else said, "I can offer
this," and another something else, until the bits became more
and more.

Marcus: It was no longer A plus B equals AB—not enough. But
it was A plus B ends up *a feast!* This reminds me of a couple of
years ago when a group of us went to El Salvador to acknowledge
the anniversary of Archbishop Oscar Romero's assassination and
to celebrate his life, we gathered in this enormous group of people
on the street for a Mass one evening. You could barely make
out—*I* could barely make out, over the tops of the heads—the
stage where the priests stood. Some people climbed trees; I was
tempted. But you could barely make out, clear across this square,
the place where the priests were leading the worship. You could
hear voices; you couldn't see who was talking, any of this kind
of stuff. It was just incredible, this enormous crowd of people
from all over the world. They went through the Mass and then
we heard the priests say, "And now we're going to serve the Eucharist. We're going to serve Communion to you." I thought,
"How is this going to happen? We've got to rehearse it when
we serve Communion to 120 people. How are they going to do
this?"

Marcia: There were thousands, tens of thousands perhaps, in
that square. Then suddenly out of nowhere, out of somewhere,
there were priests and there were Women Religious, and they

had the Eucharist in their hands and they moved out among the crowd. People were straining and crying out for it. I thought, "Oh boy, so many people are going to be disappointed. They aren't ever going to get way back here." But they *did.* They just kept moving through the crowd. "Body of Christ, body of Christ, body of Christ." *Everyone* was fed. And when they got to the back, they came back through the other way, just to make sure no one was left out. "Body of Christ, body of Christ." *Everyone was fed.*

Marcus: We talk about this story of the miracle of the loaves and fishes, but it really is more about the miracle of the *transformation of the crowd to community.* The people changed. That is what the real miracle is, in terms of this experience. It is that the *people* changed, because Jesus evoked the power and the presence of God that was in their midst. They didn't know it, and so they began to experience themselves as communion—the body of Christ.

Marcia: Perhaps that was what our invitation was six years ago (to partnership), and continues to be our invitation: to experience the Spirit of God moving among us in ways that we can't begin to predict or figure out, much less rehearse. And yet the Spirit moves among us and we become connected and related, and the bread is multiplied. The communion is there, and there is the body of Christ: feast among us.

Marcus: At our best, when we gather around this table, when we come here this morning, there is a sense in which the world really does isolate us. We end up experiencing ourselves, making it on our own, depending on our own resources to get by. When we gather here, at our best, around this table and we allow ourselves to partake of this bread and this cup, the miracle happens all over again. We are transformed, if we notice the power and the presence of God among us. Amen.

Web Visions

Marcia B. Bailey
John 16:5–16 (The Inclusive New Testament)

> Now I am going to the One who sent me—yet not one of
> you has asked, 'Where are you going?' You're sad of heart
> because I tell you this. Still, I must tell you the truth: it is
> much better for you that I go. If I fail to go, the Paraclete will
> never come to you, whereas if I go, I will send her to you.
> When she comes, she will prove the world wrong about sin,
> about justice and about judgment. About sin—in that they
> refuse to believe in me; about justice—because I go to Abba
> God and you will see me no more; about judgment—for the
> ruler of this world has been condemned. I have much more
> to tell you, but you can't bear to hear it now. When the Spirit
> of truth comes, she will guide you into all truth. She won't
> speak on her own initiative; rather, she'll speak only what she
> hears, and she'll announce to you things that are yet to come.
> In doing this, the Spirit will give glory to me, for she will take
> what is mine and reveal it to you. Everything that Abba God
> has belongs to me. This is why I said that the Spirit will take
> what is mine and reveal it to you. Within a short time you
> won't see me, but soon after that you'll see me again.

We have been talking about a new vision of the church; a new
way of being in community and being community; a new way
of thinking about each other, about ourselves, about our call
and invitation from God. We have been using this image of the
web—interconnected lines of relationship, an image of movement and dynamic energy, an image of vitality and surprises and
possibility and hope. We have been suggesting that this vision,
this image, is reflective of several things: it is reflective of what
science is telling us about creation, about the interconnectedness
of earth and sky, of plant and animal life, of humanity and the

cosmos, of how the universe is constantly expanding, of how creation is constantly in progress, of how newness is being born each and every day. We have also suggested that this vision, this image, is reflective of the invitation of God—to love and honor and value all creation as good, to embody Jesus's model of mutual leadership and shared empowerment, to anticipate the Spirit's dance of inspiration among us, to celebrate Love's inclusiveness that reflects the diversity of life.

This morning I want you to hear this vision, to see this image, as a challenge and an invitation for us, for Central Baptist Church. A challenge to reenvision who we are and what we are about, a challenge to examine how we function, how we do our work, an invitation to trust that God's Spirit will lead us into new life. It is a challenge the disciples knew something about.

John's Gospel goes to great lengths to capture something of the feel of what was taking place between Jesus and the disciples in the days and hours before his arrest. Used to traveling together, they were shocked to think that Jesus was leaving them, in spite of the variety of ways he attempted to prepare them.

Things are going to be different, he warns them. It won't look or sound or feel or be the same. But believe me when I say this: it will be better! It is for your benefit that I go. For in my place you will receive the Spirit—the Comforter, Advocate, Revealer of Truth. You will be accompanied by the Transformer, who will teach you and guide you and inspire you—who will give you life. And, although you won't see me at first, eventually you will—and you'll know then that it's me.

It's a new vision. A new image. And with these words the disciples' whole world was turned upside down—again. They had been radically transformed once—when Jesus entered their lives. And now he was expecting them to be transformed again?

This was a huge turning point. Jesus was leaving and things would be very different for them. They were used to physical, visible companionship and guidance. They now needed a new way to think about and to be in relationship with each other and with the Christ. Jesus promises them an inner companion, the Holy Spirit, who would accompany them in [the] new reality of their lives.

Jesus is quite insistent: the Spirit comes for their own, for *our* own, growth. There was no great need to exercise much faith with Jesus there in their midst, any more than there is much need for Christians today to flex their faith-muscles when nothing much out of the ordinary comes our way. When we know how everything goes, when we've figured out the answers, faith is pretty much routine, like breathing. We do it without thinking about it; it keeps us alive without effort on our part.

So what's that have to do with our web vision? Well, we too find ourselves at a turning point. Perhaps it's not as dramatic for us as it was for the disciples but the effect is very much the same. Our turning point has to do with where we find ourselves in the realities of this postmodern age. Old ways of thinking—whether two thousand or two hundred years old—just don't answer all the questions the world is asking itself today. There are new truths that need to be factored into our societal consciousness—truths about science, about humanity, about spirituality, about politics and economics, about power and justice, and about hope. The reality is our old models don't work for many of our new truths. It's like hanging onto the "earth is flat" mode when we already know it's round. We know, for example, that hierarchy and diversity are mutuality exclusive. We also know that the earth is not an inexhaustible resource for human beings' consumption. We are learning that the poor will never "pull themselves up by their bootstraps" in a global economy designed to keep them poor. Such knowledge requires a new way of thinking—about the world, about the church, about us.

You know, those who are thinking about this web vision—scientists, theologians, some managerial/business types—all seem to agree with what Jesus knew all along: "disequilibrium is the necessary condition for a system's growth."[1] Knocking something off balance leads to change, and change is necessary for growth. With enough disruption, something new begins to happen. Jesus knew that the disruption of his leaving would lead to the Spirit's coming and that would lead to growth. The question for us is: what will the disruption of our present day lead to for us?

The vision of the web is not an end in itself; the vision of the web is to be constantly spinning off more and more webs. Life creates life! Relationships invite us into more and more relationships. One of the challenges is to trust the web, and the Spirit's work within the web, to lead us to more and more life.

I've had conversation with a few of you in recent days about our going to El Salvador. "Why do we want to go?" was essentially the question being asked. And my answer has to do with the web. We go to El Salvador for many reasons—because of our history with a people and a nation struggling for justice and basic human resources, because of a shared vision with people like Carlos Sanchez, Ishmael Mendoza, Ruth and Alex Orantes—a vision of mutuality, empowerment, gender equity, spiritual transformation, justice, peace, clean water and air, education for children, food on the table. I was so excited to get home last night to read a 28-page document from Alex Orantes outlining the vision, mission, and program dreams for the congregation and community where he serves. Listen to this mission state-ment: "To accompany the communities in their struggle against hunger, poverty, and exclusion though a holistic, prophetic, and ecumenical pastoral approach that promotes human and com-munity development with a practical transforming and liberat-ing faith which generates new women and men with Christian spirituality and mystique who become organic agents of change in the communities and who contribute to the full well-being of peace with justice and dignified life as signs of the Kingdom of God amongst the poor."[2] How exciting is that? And does any of that sound like what we here are about? Of course!

Listen to what Alex writes: "Please make it known to all at Central Baptist that we love them and look forward to greeting the representatives from the church in our country. All of you mean so very much to us. You make us feel we are not alone in our work, and there is no price, no dollar amount, which will take the place of the value and worth we feel because of your solidarity and friendship which we share thus far." *This* is a web relationship!

By asking the questions together, by nurturing the relationships between us, by sharing the visions and dreams for a just and loving society, by recognizing the power and the presence of God's Holy Spirit within and among and between us, we are knit together in a communion that bridges the gulf of wealth and poverty, that diminishes the painful reality of privilege and desolation, that envisions something of the possibility of wholeness and human dignity, that bears witness to the incarnation of the living Christ.

The power of the web vision is *transformation.* I cannot be in relationship to you and not be changed. I go to El Salvador *to be changed.* I go knowing that in one way or another I will come face to face with the living Christ. I go knowing that that reality will be too much for me, that I will not be able to remain who and what I am in that Light. But I also go knowing that unless I stand in that Presence, unless I see Jesus in the eyes of these strangers-sisters-brothers, I will not become all God invites me to be, all God invites us to be.

And that's what scares the life out of some of us: the thought that we will be changed, transformed. And that's what brings life to those who dare to seek it. Change is necessary for growth. Jesus knew that. To some degree we know it too. The challenge is being willing to embrace it.

CBC has long prided itself (a dangerous word) on being different, on the cutting edge, "out there." So what's holding us back? You who said last September at our congregational meeting that you wanted to "think outside the box"—and anyone else—think about this: What would web leadership look like at CBC? What kind of structure, or lack of structure, would we fashion in response to mutuality, to shared power and ownership of the ministry God calls us to in this place? This community needs to hear what the Spirit is saying to you about this, about us.

You who said last September that children and youth should be priority—and anyone else—what implications does the web of relationships have for nurturing youth, for capturing their energy and their wisdom, for raising up another generation who have justice and love in their eyes?

And you who said last September that you were experiencing a tug of the Spirit for global concerns, for interfaith web-knitting, for economic justice—and anyone else—what opportunities in our present disequilibrium prepare us for new possibilities, new relationships, new definitions of *neighbor* and *friend*? How might we weave a web that extends across all those lines we've been told so long not to cross?

My friends, I believe the Spirit is among us, offering us a new vision and a new invitation for life! The Word is attempting to become flesh once again. Transformation is a fearful yet wonderful thing, and I am convinced that we are where we are at this moment for just this very thing. I invite you to pray deeply about this vision for your own life and for the life of our congregation. Talk to one another; think out loud. Speak the what-ifs and the why-nots to one another so that we can all hear God at work in us. This is not "my thing"; neither is it "Marcus's thing." It is *God's* thing—an invitation to a radically transformative way of being with and for each other—right here, in this church, in our families, and in the world. May we have ears to hear, eyes to see, and faith to follow.

Notes

Chapter 1

1. Susan Willhauck and Jacqulyn Thorpe, *The Web of Women's Leadership: Recasting Congregational Ministry* (Nashville: Abingdon Press, 2001), 60.

Chapter 3

1. Personal e-mail correspondence from Marcus C. Pomeroy to Marcia B. Bailey, October 24, 2006.

Chapter 4

1. Cletus Wessels, *The Holy Web: Church and the New Universe Story* (Maryknoll, NY: Orbis Books, 2000), 6.

Appendix A

1. Saville Sax and Sandra Hollander, *Reality Games: The Games People Ought to Play—A Way of Relating to Others with Greater*

Clarity, Directness and Depth (New York: The Macmillian Company, 1972), 150.

Appendix B

1. Margaret Wheatley, *Leadership and the New Science: Learning about Organization from an Orderly Universe* (San Francisco: Berrett-Koehler, 1992), 88.
2. Mission statement of Shalom Baptist Church, Atiquizaya, El Salvador.

Annotated
Bibliography

⧤For further reading on topics related to this book, you might consider:

Sofield, Loughlan and Carroll Juliano. *Collaboration: Uniting Our Gifts in Ministry.* Notre Dame, IN: Ava Maria Press, 2000.

A thoughtful book on collaboration in the context of the hierarchy of the Catholic church. Loughlan and Juliano embrace mutuality despite the given structural restrictions.

Wessels, Cletus. *The Holy Web: Church and the New Universe Story.* Maryknoll, NY: Orbis Books, 2000.

Drawing on contemporary science, Wessels connects the web of relationships with Jesus's ministry and vision for humanity.

Wheatley, Margaret J. *Leadership and the New Science: Learning about Organization from an Orderly Universe.* San Francisco: Berrett-Koehler, 1992.

Wheatley draws on new discoveries about creation's own ways of ordering and renewal to suggest organization strategies.

Wheatley, Margaret J. and Myron Kellner-Rogers. *A Simpler Way.* San Francisco: Berrett-Koehler, 1996.

Based on Wheatley's findings in *Leadership and the New Science,* this book presents creative organizational discoveries in an almost poetic style. Its pithy truths and short chapters make it accessible, and it lends itself to reflection and discussion starters.

Willhauck, Susan and Jacqulyn Thorpe. *The Web of Women's Leadership: Recasting Congregational Ministry.* Nashville: Abingdon, 2001.

This discussion of transforming hierarchy and the resulting web of relationships stops short of actually putting the model into practice.